CW00569374

Organising
Voluntary Agencies
A Guide
through the Literature

Margaret Harris
and
David Billis

BEDFORD SQUARE PRESS | NCVO

Published by
BEDFORD SQUARE PRESS of the
National Council for Voluntary Organisations
26 Bedford Square, London WC1B 3HU

© Margaret Harris and David Billis 1985

All rights reserved. No part of this publication may be
reproduced or transmitted, in any form or by any means,
electronic, mechanical, photocopying, recording or otherwise
without the prior permission of the publisher.

ISBN 0 7199 1147 8

First published 1986

Typeset by D. P. Media Limited, Hitchin, Hertfordshire

Printed and bound in England by
Biddles Ltd, Guildford and King's Lynn

Contents

Acknowledgements   v

Introduction   1

Bibliographic Entries   11

Users' Guide to Topics and Issues   113

Journals Cited   121

List of Useful Addresses   123

Contents

Introduction

Acknowledgements

We gratefully acknowledge the help that we have received at various stages in the compilation of this bibliography from: Professor Ralph Kramer, Dr James Edward Ruckle, the Brunel University Library and the NCVO Library.

The preparation of the final draft was assisted by a grant from the British Library.

Thanks are due also to Mrs Zena Pereira and Mrs Marie Heard who typed the manuscripts.

Introduction

The origins of this bibliography lie buried in a programme of research and training into voluntary action (PORTVAC) which began towards the end of 1978.[1] One of us had by then spent eight years as a member of a team engaged in collaborative research into the organisation of governmental welfare agencies – social services departments (SSDs). At that time, problems of organisation and management in those social services departments were mainly viewed as an inherent feature of large bureaucratic agencies. Little thought had been given to the possibility that the smaller, voluntary welfare agencies might have organisational problems too. Nevertheless it was, in fact, from statutory sector involvement that our own voluntary sector programme evolved. Some of the new staff appointed by SSDs were called 'voluntary liaison officers'. As a result of becoming involved in their problems, in the difficulties that departments were experiencing in integrating them into their structures, and in the difficulties that the new officers were facing in establishing the boundaries of their role, a series of research workshops was set under way. Several participants from voluntary organisations also attended these workshops. It was at this point that 'organisation and the voluntary sector' emerged as a possible distinct area of concern. For it rapidly became clear that voluntary agencies, too, had organisational and management problems.

The years since the establishment of our research programme have witnessed the role of the voluntary sector emerging as a major social policy issue. We do not intend to enter that debate here but merely to note one of its intriguing features. That is, the way in which broad-brush social policy arguments about welfare pluralism, representative democracy, individual independence and liberty, the meaning of 'community' and so on, are intertwined with concepts of an organisational character: of effectiveness, costs, flexibility, sensitivity to need etc.

Once stated, the point seems fairly obvious. *There is a link between social policy and organisation that is rarely stated, and even more rarely explored*. It is a link which, our programme suggests, is particularly strong in the voluntary welfare sector.

There are important consequences of this link for those who consider themselves to be active solely in one or other of these activities. Social policy-makers, students, researchers, funders, managers and practitioners risk losing contact with reality if they ignore the organisational

1

dimension. The risk to those researching, teaching, studying and working in the field of voluntary sector organisation is no less. For without at least an awareness of the main trends in social policy debate, they too will lose contact with the broader social reality within which voluntary agencies operate. Therefore this bibliography, although its focus is organisational, is keenly aware of the link and is addressed to all these groups.

Voluntary agencies and their problems

The establishment of PORTVAC resembled the birth of many voluntary organisations themselves. There was an obvious need, few funds were available, and nobody else seemed to be doing anything. Eventually, a sympathetic sponsor came forward and a series of workshops devoted to the specific organisational needs of voluntary agencies was launched. At the time of writing, over 100 agencies have participated in the workshops and these have been followed by 10 collaborative research projects with individual agencies.

This experience leaves us in little doubt that the voluntary sector abounds in problems. Various constellations of problems seem to emerge whenever groups of staff and committee members gather together. Surprisingly, it is not lack of funding which appears as the major organisational problem. This is of course a chronic and burning issue for most agencies, but we would argue that there are other prior and more fundamental issues which need to be addressed if full advantage is to be taken of the potential funding sources.

Coping with *organisational growth*, for example, has emerged as a greater problem than sheer organisational survival. And in those few cases where organisational survival has actually been the predominant problem, we have been able to trace back to a point where an earlier examination of the issue of growth might well have avoided current distress. Coping with growth might seem a pleasant sort of problem to handle; but it can be painful and destructive if not thought through and analysed. Sadly, we have numerous examples of agencies where funding has been snatched up without due consideration being given to the way in which some kinds of funding can distort original purposes. Thoughtless growth can alter the fundamental equations upon which the agency was established. It can alter the relationships between members and elected committees, between paid staff and membership, and between volunteer and paid staff. Finally, it can change the nature of the agency's output. Agencies can find themselves delivering services which are in fact very different from their declared objectives.

Another group of problems revolves around the role of *management committees*. There are agencies where the paid staff make the running, and in fact appoint their management committees. There are agencies that, to all intents and purposes, have no real governing body. And there are agencies where the management committee takes such an interventionist role in day-to-day operations that the work of paid staff is made virtually impossible. In some places committees meet endlessly and decide little. In others the calibre and experience of committee members is such that little could be expected from them, given the purpose of the agency. Yet in other instances we have been told by staff how much they miss the presence of a 'proper' management committee that could give appropriate guidance and support.

The role of the paid *director*, amid the confusion of the management committee position, is often a difficult one. In many cases there is no clear statement of what sort of role the director should play. Should he or she just keep things ticking along, or are there expectations of a more dynamic and forward-looking approach? Should he co-ordinate or actively lead? Should he represent the public face of the agency or be directed towards managing the organisation? The boundary between the director's work and that of the management committee is, for many agencies, exceedingly unclear.

Several agencies do not evaluate whether a gap has developed between their *stated policies* and *actual implementation*. In a number of the collaborative research projects, where we had the opportunity to study these matters in greater depth, it could be seen how, over the years, agency policies had congealed into positions which were not really capable of implementation. The consequences of this gap between policy and implementation were widespread and damaging. Much time and effort can be invested in the pursuit of fantasy policies. In such situations it is questionable whether all this effort was really as productive as it might have been. Furthermore, in other areas, such as *recruitment* and *training*, confusion was reinforced by the selection of inappropriate staff who were thereafter trained towards implementing unrealistic policies. The end-product of all this was considerable staff unease and unhappiness.

The *internal structure of accountability* of many agencies is confused. This is a matter of some concern since it is often impossible to know who really is accountable for what action and for what expenditure. We must assume that this is of dubious benefit to clients. But even if this point must remain unproven, there will, we imagine, be a limit to the benevolent non-involvement of the external funders. There is a link here between internal and external accountability which has not, so far, attracted much attention. As the voluntary sector takes a more prominent place in the provision of social welfare, so too can we expect a greater scrutiny of its internal affairs by statutory or private funders.

There is another major area of problems which might be described as

3

resulting from the tension between the formal and informal provision of services within the same agency. This is sometimes described in the literature as the problem of *formalisation* or *bureaucratisation*. We have analysed this issue elsewhere,[2] and for the purposes of this introduction one typical example might perhaps suffice. We have in mind one group of single-parent families which steadily increased its number of paid staff and subsequently faced severe conflicts between its members, who wished (in the main) to retain the informal self-help character of the group, and the staff who desired to provide a service to a wider range of people.[3] Of course, there are always close inter-relationships between problem areas. In this case, formalisation could be seen as part of the general category of policy confusion or growth. Nevertheless, it is sufficiently widespread and important to deserve mention as a problem in its own right.

There are other issues which could be mentioned in order to illustrate the wide range of organisational problems in the voluntary sector. There is the question of *professionalisation* of voluntary work, the role of *trade unions*, the relationships between *headquarters and geographically dispersed units*, *charismatic leadership*, problems of *recruitment*, *training and career progression*, and many more.

In presenting this account of some of the organisational problems facing voluntary agencies we must emphasise in the strongest possible fashion that our purpose is not to paint an unduly pessimistic picture of what is happening inside those agencies. That our account is a fair reflection of reality is supported by other evidence such as the presentations made at the 1982 Annual Conference of the Association of Researchers into Voluntary Action (ARVAC), and the Handy Report.[4]

However, this evidence of organisational problems also suggests that the sector is doing things that it is rightly valued for. So we do not in any way wish to deny the positive character of voluntary agencies or their employees, governors and volunteers. The claim that we are making is that *many of these initiatives can be more effectively and efficiently undertaken*. In this connection we would like to note in passing the tendency, in some agencies, to attribute all organisational ills to problems of 'personality'. To those who still believe that this can be the major cause, we can only point out that the problems we list appear too widespread, and follow too many similar patterns, to be explained solely by accidents of personality. We must look instead to the possibility of more fundamental structural problems of the sort we have already noted: growth, the role of management committees and staff, policy clarification and implementation, authority and accountability. In most areas of organisational life in other sectors, and on an international level, it is now accepted that we have little choice but to seek organisation and management tools, however crude, which might help us understand the complexities of working together.

The search for ideas

We have so far briefly described the background to our research programme (PORTVAC) and outlined some of its areas of concern. It is now necessary to delineate the context of this bibliography. In brief, this was set by the organisational problems that were revealed by our programme. This present work might therefore be regarded as a search for ideas and theories, which might serve some useful purpose for those who, in one way or another, have to be aware of, and respond to, those problems.

In this search we have attempted to maintain a balanced approach towards the role of the voluntary sector in the provision of welfare. The stick which is currently (1985) being used to beat the back of governmental provision could easily turn to an alternative target. If the voluntary sector aids and abets the raising of community expectations beyond what is reasonable and possible, it too can expect the inevitable backlash. In making this point we do no more than raise warning signals. Some of the lessons of our research so far, as briefly discussed in the previous section, do indeed suggest that a balanced and cautious approach might be a prudent standpoint.

We have tried to extend a balanced approach not only to the role of the voluntary sector, but also to the available material on organisation and management. Naturally, given the historical role of the state in the organised provision of welfare in this country, we began the search for material with the benefit of a substantial body of knowledge drawn from our own research in the public as well as private sectors. However, there is an unsatisfactory limit to the light that is thrown on voluntary sector organisational problems by any pre-existing body of knowledge. The challenge that faces researchers and practitioners is to find new ideas *which draw their strength from the specific conditions of the voluntary sector*, and which will in turn, we believe, provide more satisfactory answers to the problems of the sector. It was in a modest effort to come to grips with that challenge that we embarked on this bibliography.

Boundaries to the bibliography

We have now discussed the context and the approach of this bibliography, and in so doing we hope that we have provided a reasonable outline of our focus. However, we are aware that we have as yet said little about the types of voluntary agencies included in the bibliography, although the earlier descriptions of the problems encountered may give a fairly good idea of the broad category of agencies that are our concern. We have also said nothing about the sources we have chosen, although

5

once again we hope that the previous sections will have provided an implicit explanation for the choice of source material. So in this section we will briefly discuss various choices that we had to make, and in so doing we will establish a rough framework for the bibliography.

We believe it is fair to claim that this is a pioneering venture in the sense that it draws together material, and attempts to establish a boundary, around an area of study which is generally agreed to be important, but in which there are very few distinctive or specific works. Our bibliography reflects the wide-ranging characteristics of this new field insofar as we could not simply provide a listing of existing material. We had, rather, to examine a very wide range of writings which, often as part of their prime concern, seemed to us to say something of relevance to this new field of study. Thus, in the search for useful material, we have moved across the traditional academic disciplines.

A first boundary to this project was set by our own research programme in which we were primarily concerned with voluntary agencies working broadly in the social welfare field which employ at least some paid staff. So, in selecting references for this bibliography we focused, in the main, on material that was specifically concerned, or was closely associated with, these kinds of agencies. Thus with a few exceptions of works that we felt might shed some light on the formal-informal tension discussed on pages 3–4, we have generally not included works from the literature on volunteering, self-help and community.

In the light of the challenge to find new and useful ideas mentioned earlier, it seemed appropriate to concentrate on material that, in our judgement, had something original, telling, or useful to say about organising voluntary agencies. At the beginning of our project we had intended to include only empirical or research-based material. But such is the paucity of British research into the organisational problems of voluntary agencies that our criterion of usefulness has caused us to include 'impressionistic' and 'journalistic' articles if we felt that they could make a useful contribution to knowledge. Taking into account our two criteria of specific concern and usefulness, we excluded most of the general organisation and management literature.

We also excluded much of the more detailed technical literature on matters such as fund-raising techniques, employment law, accounting procedures and running meetings. Umbrella bodies, including most notably the NCVO, have in recent years produced a number of handbooks and guides to these kinds of topics. So we felt it better to concentrate on broader organisation and management issues where access to the relevant literature is more problematic.

The third boundary with regard to source material was to include, in general, works that are publicly available. That is to say, that they are for sale in the U.K., are available in libraries, or appear in journals which the reader may have some reasonable hope of securing. In general, we have not included publications which agencies themselves produced, or which are primarily intended for a particular specialised agency or group of agencies. Undoubtedly, in setting this boundary, we may have done some injustice to significant writings which would have contributed to the general aim of this bibliography.

Another criterion was set by date of publication. We have concentrated on relevant literature produced in the last ten years or so, up to the end of 1984. Older material has only been included if it was felt that it retained usefulness and immediacy despite the passage of time.

There is another important boundary which needs some explanation. We have deliberately extended the range of our interests beyond the confines of British writings on the subject. In the last year or so, through our work in PORTVAC, we have become aware of a number of other international foci of similar interests. We do not pretend in any way to have identified all those students in other countries who are also concerned with the organisational aspects of voluntary agencies. But there was one obvious centre of writing which we could hardly ignore if we were to meet our stated objective of extending the range of ideas and thoughts on these issues. We refer of course, to the North American literature. Whilst a truly comprehensive coverage could not be entertained, and might never in fact be feasible, we have nevertheless established contact with several key writers in the area who were generous in their help in identifying what might be considered to be significant literature.

There are, however, difficulties with North American literature. In particular we must remember that the voluntary sector in North America bears a larger share of total responsibility for the provision of welfare than in this country. On the other hand, American writers frequently do not distinguish between voluntary and governmental auspices when discussing organisational aspects of human services. Therefore, the extent of the applicability of their writings to the British scene may be unclear.

There are other difficulties, as well. The terms 'third sector' and 'non-profit organisations' are frequently used in American literature; but neither of these is identical with our own 'voluntary sector'. The former term generally refers to all those organisations which are not part of either the governmental or the private commercial sector, and includes (in addition to voluntary welfare agencies) clubs and associations, self-help groups, and pressure groups. The second term, 'non-profit organisatons' (or the 'not-for-profit' sector) includes all those organisations which do not have as their primary goal the making of profits. The

7

term thus embraces most of the governmental sector as well as the 'third sector'. Yet another terminological difficulty may arise over the American use of the term 'voluntary associations' to refer to groups, clubs and self-help groups; sometimes to service-delivering agencies, and sometimes to a combination of both.

But despite these terminological problems which reflect the different British and North American perspectives, we feel that the inclusion of some writings from Canada and the USA has enriched the bibliography. For the same reason, we have included a few references to readily-available material from Australia and India.

To summarise, the rough boundaries of this enquiry were set by:

- the focus on social welfare agencies employing at least some paid staff
- our judgement on the contribution of the material to knowledge about the organisation of voluntary agencies
- the availability of the material
- the age of the material
- our desire to draw (with caution) on the experience of other countries, especially the United States

This guide through the literature is, therefore, highly selective and very much an exploration based on our personal evaluation of what might be useful to those concerned with the organisation and management of the voluntary sector. One result of this approach is that many of the classics of the voluntary sector literature are given little attention, whilst some little-known papers are given prominence. At this stage in the development of research interest in the field we saw no other alternative. As each article and book was weighed for possible inclusion, we were forced to define and redefine for ourselves a viable boundary to our enterprise. We have judged candidates for inclusion against the background of our research experience, and we have added brief personal observations to help guide the reader through new and uncertain terrain.

The end-product does not resemble a traditional bibliography. We have eschewed detached abstracts or overviews in favour of more selective descriptions coupled with our own judgements where appropriate. And, since many of the entries deal with more than one organisational theme, we have not grouped them by subject matter but have preferred a more neutral alphabetical listing by author. We hope that the resulting format, supplemented by the Users' Guide and the alphabetical List of Titles, will meet the needs of our readers and allow them to enter this book at any point, according to their own interests and perspectives.

The format of this book

Entries with comment

In searching for material it seemed that some items were particularly useful and relevant. In general, these are the lengthiest entries and include our own brief comments which are separated from the main text of the entry by a line. (For example, see the entry on the *Lovelock Report*.) These comments note, where appropriate,

- the relevance of the entry to problems
- whether it raises important issues
- whether it contributes to theory development
- its relationship, if any, to other literature.

The first paragraphs of these longer entries explain the initial aim or focus of the source material, and the relevant findings or problems exposed by the author. They do not represent abstracts or paraphrases, but are intended to draw attention to the key organisational points raised. Key topics and issues appear in *italics* and are also listed separately on pages 113–119. Where materials are unlikely to be easily obtainable in libraries, the address of the publisher or sponsoring institution is given or the abbreviation 'ILL' is used to indicate that the material is available via Inter-Library Loan.

Shorter entries

We also came across many other writings which we felt did not warrant such detailed attention. We have included them but, in general, they are shorter entries and we have not added any comments of our own. Many of these are well-known or frequently-referenced books and articles in the voluntary sector field which, nevertheless, bear only peripherally or indirectly on our own present specific interest. Others are examples of material which fell just outside our chosen boundaries, peripheral material which deserved at least to be brought to the attention of those concerned with the organisation of the voluntary sector. Finally, some entries comprise writings whose titles suggest an organisational focus, but which, on examination, were found to be less useful. We hoped to save readers' time by indicating the true nature of their content. And, of course, some references carry only short commentaries because, although interesting, they were judged not weighty enough to justify detailed analysis.

Users' guide

In line with our main objective, which was to draw together useful ideas and theories, we have added a Users' Guide to the material. This guide is not intended as a comprehensive index. Its purpose is to provide some *initial* references and ideas for those readers who wish to explore particular topics.

In conclusion

The preparation of this bibliography has enabled us to start mapping the field of a new area of interest and study. Inevitably, we may have excluded works which others regard as important, or given what might be seen as undue prominence to individual works. We would therefore warmly welcome users' comments and also their suggestions for inclusion in any future edition of this bibliography.

Notes

1. The Brunel University Programme of Research and Training into Voluntary Action (PORTVAC).
2. D. Billis, *Research and Practice in Voluntary Sector Management*, PORTVAC Working Paper 1, Brunel University, 1984.
3. D. Billis, *Self-Help and Service*, PORTVAC Working Paper 2, Brunel University, 1984.
4. B. Knight (ed), *Management in Voluntary Organisations*, ARVAC Occasional Paper No. 6, 1984. Report of the Charles Handy Working Party on *Improving Effectiveness in Voluntary Organisations*, Bedford Square Press/NCVO, 1981. Further evidence of this contention can be seen in the stream of more impressionistic articles which constantly appear in the press.

Bibliographic Entries

P. Abrams, *Neighbourhood Care and Social Policy: A Research Perspective*, Occasional Paper, Volunteer Centre, 1978 (1).

In this booklet, Abrams uses a study of a good neighbour scheme as a basis for a discussion of the broader context and implications of neighbourhood care. He defines neighbourhood care as 'a local organisation of voluntary (and to a lesser degree, statutory) efforts to provide support in diverse forms for those who have fallen through the net of the system of informal care'.

The good neighbour scheme studied was located in a 'zone of transition' and a traditional working class area. The scheme in fact lacked clients. The volunteers were regarded by local people as a 'gratuitous intrusion': people who differed from others not in their readiness to give care but in their self-importance and demand for public recognition of their helpfulness. The nature of the care needs in the area were not congruent with what the helpers were able to give; for example, helpers did not want to get too involved. Thus, needs remained unmet and volunteers were disillusioned and wasted. The formal organisation of the scheme was good but it was not able to build a bridge into the existing informal caring networks.

In analysing the problems revealed by the study, Abrams suggests that there are two fundamentally different drives that are probably incompatible. One drive is towards the extension of the welfare state and entails formal social action. But there is also a pull towards the extension of neighbourliness which builds on informal social relationships. Because the private sector of informal relations persistently fails to provide enough care for enough people, the public sector tends to colonise the private sector, to invade and reorganise it so that public sector standards of effective care can be more thoroughly realised. It does this either by attempting to support and regenerate caring agents in the informal sector, or by reconstructing and supplanting informal care in terms of its own conceptions of effectiveness. At present the voluntary provision of neighbourhood care straddles both these approaches.

Abrams argues that four bases for offering care may be discerned: altruism or beneficence; tradition; self-importance; and reciprocity. Informal caring in the community is rooted in a special sort of reciprocity. It *can* be renewed through social policy, but this depends on finding the means of 'giving people opportunities to engage in caring relationships'.

The theme of tension between the formal and informal worlds has emerged in other writings about the voluntary sector (see, for example, *Lundberg, Twelvetrees* and *van der Eyken*) and has been developed in *Billis, 1984* (1).

Other aspects of organising neighbourhood care schemes, including the matching of need to manpower resources and the development of informal care, are given more detailed attention in *Abrams et al, 1981*.

P. Abrams, 'Community Care: Some Research Problems and Priorities', in J. Barnes and N. Connelly (eds), *Social Care Research*, Bedford Square Press/NCVO, 1978 (2).

The main focus of this paper is on the idea of community care and the conceptual problems raised by research projects in this area. However, it also touches on some themes which are of concern to practitioners in voluntary agencies; these include the conditions conducive to caring activity; the importance of reciprocity in caring relationships; and the question of spontaneity. As regards this latter, Abrams argues that there is no evidence 'that spontaneity is in any way an important source of the type of sustained altruistic practice which community care embodies'. As elsewhere (for example, in *Abrams, 1978* (1)) he argues that the 'relevant distinction is between formal and informal organisation, *not* between organisation and spontaneity'.

P. Abrams, 'Social Change, Social Networks and Neighbourhood Care', *Social Work Service*, 22 February 1980, pp. 12–23.

This article develops some of the themes of the author's earlier paper (*Abrams, 1978* (1)). It draws on studies of neighbourhood care schemes to illustrate the distinction between informal and formal methods of caring.

P. Abrams, S. Abrams, R. Humphrey and R. Snaith, *Action for Care: A Review of Good Neighbour Schemes in England*, Volunteer Centre, 1981.

This book is the final report of a study of 1026 good neighbour schemes, groups or organisations which 'could be described as organised attempts to mobilise local residents to increase the amount or range of help and care they give to one another'.

As regards the organisational characteristics of schemes, the researchers found great diversity. 'Indeed, were it not for their distinctive purpose of creating neighbourliness, it would be almost impossible to tell Good Neighbour Schemes apart from all the other caring projects based on voluntary visiting.' They suggest that the administrative diversity they found reflects 'a tension between dispersal and centralisation caused by the fact that the schemes are committed simultaneously to providing care and to promoting neighbourliness'. Efficient performance of tasks seems to demand centralised service-management whereas 'getting people involved' has a decentralising logic.

The researchers found a dramatic regional maldistribution of schemes relative to need indicators. Schemes were concentrated in the South-East. It seems that the incidence of schemes reflects the availability of helpers and organisers, rather

12

than social environment. Schemes developed most readily in prosperous areas where there was a supply of women who did not work and who could carry the costs of their voluntary involvement.

The most successful schemes were those whose organisers devoted much effort to matching the aptitudes and wishes of available helpers to the two different kinds of work involved in good neighbour schemes, i.e. neighbourly contact and the performance of specific caring tasks.

In their relationships with statutory organisations, schemes encountered the problem of maintaining 'dialogue without control'. This was particularly acute as many good neighbour schemes were dependent for their survival on referrals and grants from statutory agencies.

This book raises an issue which is particularly relevant for voluntary agencies in the early stages of growth; even when the aim of a group is to encourage informal caring relationships, it seems that 'if it is to succeed it must be based on carefully thought out formal arrangements and strategies'. Goals are achieved through 'a determined organisational effort' rather than by muddling through.

S. Abrams: see p. 12.

The Accountant, 'Charities', Supplement to *The Accountant*, Vol. 187, 16 December 1982, pp. 850–860.

This supplement contains three articles about charities; two about the problems of accounting in charities and one about discretionary covenants.

Accounting Standards Committee (ASC), *Accounting by Charities: ASC Discussion Paper*, **ASC, 1984. (Obtainable from Institute of Chartered Accountants in England and Wales.)**

This discussion paper derives from a working party set up to consider financial reporting by charities. It explores 'ways of enhancing the usefulness of charities' annual reports and the possibility of reducing the diverse practices of financial accounting and reporting adopted by charities'. It follows the study by *Bird and Morgan-Jones*.

T. Acton, 'Charities and the Iron Law of Chaos', *New Society*, **21 November 1974, pp. 477–479.**

This article discusses the 'extreme internal political instability' which characterises new-style campaigning charities, including the CND in the 1950s, the Campaign Against Racial Discrimination in the 1960s, and Shelter and the

Simon Community in the 1970s. Divisions arose between lobbyists and protesters, metropolitan and provincial groups, volunteers and professionals, elitists and democrats. The author argues that 'in a single-issue coalition with no prospects of overall power' people are quick to voice dissent. Thus, internal democracy will destroy every attempt to achieve overall direction or bureaucratic supervision; this is 'an Iron Law of Chaos'.

I. Allen: see p. 90.

R. N. Anthony, 'Can Non-Profit Organisations be Well Managed?', in D. Borst and P. Montana (eds), *Managing Non-Profit Organisations*, AMACOM, New York, 1977. (ILL)

This introductory chapter to *Borst and Montana*'s collection recognises the difficulties of measuring performance and the existence of political considerations in organisations in which profit-making is not the prime objective. But Anthony suggests that, nevertheless, improvements in management could be made through the application of modern management methods, higher rewards for management skills, increased competition between agencies and a firmer role for governing bodies.

R. N. Anthony and R. Herzlinger, *Management Control in Non-Profit Organisations*, Richard D. Irwin, Inc., Homewood, Illinois, 1975. (ILL)

The focus of this book is on the application of techniques of management control to non-profit organisations of all kinds.

J. Arnold, D. Askins, R. Davies, S. Evans, A. Rogers and T. Taylor, *The Management of Detached Work*, National Association of Youth Clubs, 1981.

This book is aimed at those 'involved in the processes of setting up, managing or assisting detached youth work projects', but the authors suggest that much of the book 'can be equally applied to any form of youth work or any type of management'.

Part I explores practical management issues using 'XY analysis', a way of describing relationships in terms of the relative balance within them of X qualities (natural child) and Y qualities (authoritarian parent).

The second part of the work provides a four-step guide to setting up a detached youth work project.

The 'XY analysis' which underpins all the discussions in the first part of this book does not always succeed in communicating complicated ideas in a simple way. Nevertheless, the book contains many practical suggestions for tackling and

14

avoiding the organisational problems which can arise in specially-funded projects which have their own management committees and employ professional workers.

D. Askins: see p. 15.

D. Askins: see p. 15.

Association of County Councils: see p. 15.

Association of County Councils: see p. 15.

Association of Metropolitan Authorities, National Council for Voluntary Organisations and Association of County Councils, *Working Together: Partnerships in Local Social Service*, **Bedford Square Press/NCVO, 1981.**

This booklet contains the report of a Working Party set up in October 1980 by the AMA, the ACC and NCVO 'to consider the practical aspects of the working relationships between local authority personal social services and local voluntary organisations and community groups and to identify and offer guidance on the principles and procedures which will sustain these relationships'.

The report opens with a discussion of grant-aid to voluntary agencies by local authorities and of the considerations which should inform local authorities' decisions on funding and types of funding. It argues that both local authorities and management committees of voluntary agencies should be more aware of the liabilities of voluntary agencies. Management committees, although often 'the most truly voluntary element in voluntary projects' often lack the time or skill to exercise their management functions.

As regards necessary training in management and social work skills, the report offers some practical suggestions about sharing facilities between the statutory and voluntary sectors.

Its conclusions include the following suggestions. Cooperation is required between local authorities and voluntary agencies in respect not only of operational activities but also of policy development and planning. Effective liaison structures are needed in which both parties are clear about their respective roles and ground rules are established beforehand for dealing with disputes. Participation by local authority nominees in the management of voluntary agencies 'should be kept to a minimum consistent with the accountability of the local authority for its expenditure' and should happen 'by mutual agreement'.

This book takes a *pragmatic approach*. Whatever aspect of the statutory-voluntary partnership is being discussed: grant-aid, sharing of resources, training or liaison, the approach is always to clarify the important issues and options and then to express unequivocal opinions about the most appropriate courses of action.

M. Austin and J. Posnett, 'The Charity Sector in England and Wales –
Characteristics and Public Accountability', *National Westminster Bank
Quarterly Review*, August 1979, pp. 40–51, and M. Austin and J. Posnett,
'Charitable Activity in England and Wales', *Social Policy and Administration*, 13, 3, Autumn 1979, pp. 171–185.

These articles report a study of a sample of charity accounts for the year 1975.
The authors review the main conditions of charitable status and the legal and
fiscal concessions accorded to recognised charities. They go on to emphasise the
importance of information about charities being readily available to the public
and the Charity Commissioners since, unlike other firms, charities have 'no body
of owners or shareholders to whom they are responsible for their operation'.
Donors and recipients have no statutory rights. Unless the charity is a registered
Company, the onus of control and regulation lies heavily on the trustees or
managers and on the Charity Commissioners.

In this study, 418 of the 119,978 charities registered with the Charity Commissioners in England and Wales in 1975 were sampled. Forty per cent had not filed
accounts with the Commissioners as required, and those accounts that were filed
were often very much out-of-date. Some charities were untraceable and others
refused to give their accounts when approached direct. Often accounts were
difficult to interpret because of the lack of standardised conventions. The authors
suggest that 'Taken overall this evidence suggests that the information available
to the public, or to the Charity Commissioners, is by no means comprehensive
. . . and this lack of accountability is not restricted to small charities'.

Nevertheless, the authors were able to identify some characteristics of the
charity sector. Between 1971 and 1977, the number of new charities registered
each year rose from 769 to 1830. Poverty relief is declining in relative importance
among new charities; social welfare and culture are their most popular objectives.
In 1975, two-thirds of the total income of registered charities was contributed
towards health and education causes, including independent schools. Organisations whose aims were the relief of poverty constituted 32.8 per cent of all
charities but received only 4.3 per cent of total charitable income. The top 5 per
cent of charities received 83 per cent of the total income. Forty-five per cent of
charities had income of less than £100 p.a.

The charitable sector is dominated by a relatively small number of large and
active charities serving a limited number of objects of which education is the most
important. The authors estimated that in 1975 the total charitable income
received (including that of non-registered charities) amounted to £4,159 million,
or 4.3 per cent of GNP.

A more complex and up to date picture of the charitable sector can be obtained by
considering this article alongside the work of *Gerard, 1983*, and the publications
of the NCVO and the Charities Aid Foundation. Issues about the public
accountability of the charity sector have been discussed also by *Mullin* and *T.
Yeo*.

Aves Committee Report, *The Voluntary Worker in the Social Services*, Bedford Square Press/NCVO, 1969.

This book is the report of a committee set up in 1966 'to enquire into the role of voluntary workers in the social services and in particular to consider their need for preparation or training and their relationship with professional social workers'. Its focus is on the use of volunteers by local authority social services departments and the practical and professional problems which may arise. Voluntary agencies are mentioned only in relation to their role in obtaining and organising volunteers for the statutory services.

N. Babchuk: see p. 38.

Barclay Working Party, *Social Workers: Their Role and Tasks*, Bedford Square Press/NCVO, 1982.

This is the report of a Working Party set up in October 1980, at the request of the Secretary of State for Social Services, by the National Institute for Social Work under the chairmanship of Peter Barclay. The terms of reference were 'to review the role and tasks of social workers in local authority social service departments and related voluntary agencies in England and Wales and to make recommendations'.

The first part of the report, 'The Practice of Social Work', describes what social workers do and are needed to do, as well as some of the staffing problems involved. A chapter entitled 'Social Work and the Voluntary Sector' discusses the relative contributions of the statutory and voluntary (including informal caring) sectors and suggests that statutory and voluntary services should be seen as complementary; that 'a partnership should be developed between them allowing joint planning and agreed distribution of tasks'. Use of Purchase of Service Contracts (POSC) should be further explored.

A second section, entitled 'The Context of Social Work', discusses the economic, social policy and values contexts of social work practice. A chapter on 'Issues of Organisation and Management' concentrates on matters relating to the organisation and management of local authority social services. The need for voluntary bodies to have effective organisational structures is recognised and is presented as being particularly important in the light of the authors' own advocacy of a greater degree of partnership between the statutory and voluntary sectors.

S. Bates (compiler), *Fundraising and Grant Aid for Voluntary Organisations: A Guide to the Literature*, Bedford Square Press/NCVO, 1981.

This booklet is a practical guide to publications on fund-raising and grant aid. A subject index directs readers to sources of information on specific aspects of funding.

17

M. Bayley, *Community-orientated Systems of Care*, Occasional Paper, Volunteer Centre, 1978.

This booklet provides a bibliography of issues and case studies relevant to community care.

J. Bazalgette: see p. 81.

P. E. Bebbington, 'The Efficacy of Alcoholics Anonymous: The Elusiveness of Hard Data', *British Journal of Psychiatry*, 128, pp. 572–580, 1976.

This article is not about organisational or managerial efficacy. It is concerned with the methodological difficulties of studying the effectiveness of what AA does for 'clients' or 'members' in view of its principle of confidentiality and no record-keeping.

C. Bemrose, 'The Multinational Charity Business', *Multinational Business*, 2, 1981, pp. 32–44.

This article discusses the relationship between charities and private business in the developing world. It points out their common interests in economic development and education and questions some of the stereotypes of charities as amateurish and inefficient.

C. Bennett, 'Powerless Management Committees?' *MDU Bulletin*, 2, September 1983, pp. 4–5.

Drawing on seven years' experience on the management committee of a voluntary hostel and on research into a number of similar hostels, the author of this article discusses the feelings of powerlessness which many such committees have.

She attributes these feelings to many factors. Original members are appointed for their status and fund-raising abilities rather than their managerial skills. They are confused about their role and deferential to the professional expertise of staff. Sometimes, she says, 'believing oneself powerless can be a way of justifying poor performance'.

She concludes that management committees need more self-confidence. 'Management committees which recognise their power and accept the responsibilities it entails have the potential to overcome other influences in the pursuit of what they believe to be right for their organisation.'

W. E. Berg and R. Wright, 'Program Funding As an Organizational Dilemma: Goal Displacement in Social Work Programs', *Administration and Social Work*, 4, 4, Winter 1980, pp. 29–39.

This article reports a study which investigated the possible effects on the integrity and goals of a voluntary agency of the desire or need to obtain outside funding for programmes and projects.

The authors suggest two important parameters of funding relationships; the degree of accountability required by funders and whether grants are block-grants or service-based. In service-based funding, goals are defined in relation to specified units of service to a target population; whereas for block-grants, goals are defined in relation to specified social problems. The most autonomous relationships are hypothesised to be those with a block-funding base and low accountability to funders; the most dependent relationships (in which agency goal displacement is most likely) are hypothesised to be those with high accountability to funders and a service-funding base.

The authors studied four social work programmes initiated under block-grants which later shifted to service-funding. They found that under service-based funding, agencies were 'forced to expand their client base in order to off-set the effect of a unit-cost structure that is based upon minimum rather than average or maximum estimate of expenses involved in providing services and in order to distribute the overhead costs involved in maintaining the service-based accountability system over a wider base'. The shifts in the quality and type of service provided by agencies were associated with the funding process, rather than with deliberative 'reconsideration of agency goals and objectives'.

They conclude that 'any funding agreement that requires strict and ongoing accountability and that provides funds as remuneration for units of service will tend to limit the degrees of freedom available to the agency'.

In debates in this country about the expansion of the voluntary sector role and the funding of voluntary agencies, little attention has been paid to the possible effects on voluntary agencies themselves of such expansion. Nevertheless, this is an issue which is of importance to those running voluntary agencies. The setting up of the *Lovelock* enquiry into the CAB service, for example, illustrated that the management of publicly-funded voluntary agencies cannot be divorced from a consideration of sponsors' wishes. North American experience of the effects of public funding may provide some useful lessons for Britain. *Hartogs and Weber, 1978*, and *Kramer, 1979 (2)*, reached fairly optimistic conclusions from their studies; that government funding was not inherently 'goal-corrupting'. *Berg and Wright's* more detailed analysis of different kinds of funding processes suggests that the issue is more complex and that the effects on an agency's goals of outside funding are likely to vary according to the exact nature of the arrangements made.

E. Berman, 'Voluntary Means Business', *Charity and Appeals Directory 1984: Supplement to the Law Society's Gazette*, 23 November 1983.

In this introductory article, the Founder and Chief Executive of Inter-Action Trust points to the quiet revolution that is taking place in contemporary society in the nature of charitable and voluntary endeavour. Many new voluntary agencies are in fact small not-for-profit businesses, but they lack the management skills necessary for running such enterprises.

The author concludes that, 'Funds for training/education in these skills are needed as a priority in order to maximise the benefits of all other giving. Voluntary may mean not-for-profit business, but it can only mean effective business if it can manage better what is given to it, and if givers can manage to give with more specific goals in mind.'

D. Billis, *Voluntary Organisations: Management Issues I*, PORTVAC, Brunel University, 1979.

This document is a report of the first two-day seminar organised by Brunel University's Programme of Research and Training Into Voluntary Action (PORTVAC).

The objectives of the seminar were to present and develop ideas for under-standing the organisation and management problems of voluntary organisations.

There are three main sections to the report: the problems confronting volun-tary organisations; a summary of the material presented by the course organisers; and a note of key points made in the discussion.

The list of initial problems raised was divided into three main groupings concerned with overall objectives, organisational structure, and relationships with governing bodies. Under the first heading were included problems of changing objectives, growth, boundaries with other agencies, and values. Included under the second heading (organisational structure) were problems associated with the clarification of organisational roles and internal structures, recruitment, training and career development, teamwork and motivation, pro-fessionalisation, and the maintenance of standards. The final group of problems was concerned with issues surrounding the relationship with governing bodies such as trustees and management committees.

The second section of the paper consists of summary notes of staff presenta-tions. One paper describes a theory of levels of decision-making developed by the author and a colleague in work with governmental welfare agencies.

The final section contains extracts from the discussions in which workshop participants interacted with the course tutors in the analysis of the initial prob-lems presented. An attempt is made to identify those features that might be distinctive to voluntary organisations. Among these the author identifies the phenomenon of what is called the 'overlapping triangle' – that is to say, the overlapping roles of governing bodies and employees.

20

This document is a report of one of the earliest attempts in this country to gather together a group of senior staff from voluntary agencies with the specific purpose of discussing their organisational problems. Its main interest lies in the display of the wide range of difficulties such organisations can face, and in its attempt *to develop theory* which relates to the specific characteristics of voluntary agencies. The progress of these ideas, including recognition of the phenomenon of 'overlap', can be seen in *Billis, 1984 (1)*.

D. Billis, 'The Missing Link: Some challenges for research and practice in voluntary sector management', in B. Knight (ed), *Management in Voluntary Organisations*, Occasional Paper No. 6, Association of Researchers into Voluntary Action (ARVAC), 1984 (1).

In a paper originally prepared for the 1982 Annual Conference of the Association of Researchers into Voluntary Action, the author suggests that the stereotype of the non-bureaucratic, flexible, cost-effective, and responsive voluntary agency fails to take sufficient account of the management dimension in the voluntary sector – the 'missing link' of the title. He suggests that research in this area will not only benefit clients and agency staff, it will also have an impact on the broader policy debate about the role of the voluntary sector in welfare services. After discussing some of the major problems that have emerged from the Brunel University research programme, an explanatory model is presented.

The first part of the paper argues that the problems facing voluntary sector managers are both complex and distinctive. Examples are provided of different types and intensities of problems arising in the voluntary, as compared with the statutory, sector. The author suggests that these distinctive problems require a distinctive explanatory model which would underpin research and generate new ideas. Drawing on the work of the anthropologist Edmund Leach, he develops a model in which many agencies in the voluntary sector are seen as occupying an ambiguous zone between the bureaucratic and private worlds. The validity of the model is illustrated by comparing the main definitional characteristics of bureaucracy with those of voluntary organisations. Thus the following statuses are briefly examined in relation to bureaucratic and voluntary organisations:

- *employer* and *employee*
- *employee* and *non-employee*
- *providers* and *recipients*
- *chairman* and *director*
- *director* and *managers*
- *managers* and *subordinates*.

This work pursues and develops a number of themes raised in the author's earlier paper (*Billis, 1979*). In particular, the 'overlapping triangles' of the earlier paper are taken several stages further in an attempt to explore the specific organisational characteristics of many voluntary agencies. The author offers his own tentative *model* that can be applied to help understanding of the particular

21

complexities of voluntary sector management. This paper forms the basis for D. Billis, *Research and Practice in Voluntary Sector Management*, PORTVAC Working Paper 1, Brunel University, 1984.

D. Billis, *Self-Help and Service: An Action-Research Study with a Group of One-Parent Families*, PORTVAC Working Paper 2, Brunel University, 1984 (2).

This paper reports a collaborative action-research project with 'Riverside' – a group of one-parent families. The researcher was invited in after Riverside had gone through a period of rapid change, developing from a self-help group for single parents into 'a complex organisation employing a significant number of staff who had become increasingly unclear regarding key elements of their organisational position'.

Interviews with the researcher suggested several clusters of organisational problems. There were issues surrounding the role of the governing bodies and worries about the group's increasing commitments. Personality clashes and role conflicts were noted and there was concern about lack of accountability. But the researcher felt that there was one central issue which also had implications for most of the others; that was 'a tension or conflict between the image of Riverside primarily as a self-help group or, alternatively, as a service-providing agency'.

Two possible alternative models, of 'self-help' or 'community service', were developed, drawing on the experiences of the group. The models differed with regard to membership, main purpose, staffing, budget, organisational structure, and type and style of governance. The two models were used by Riverside as a basis on which to clarify their organisational structure and implement change.

The author concludes by reflecting on the lessons of the study for the links between social policy and organisation. If, as the case study suggests, there is a basic organisational tension between self-help and service models of welfare provision, it might work to the detriment of clients and staff.

This case study provides an example of how *organisational change* might be achieved in a voluntary sector context; that is, by analysing problems as they appear to participants or members and developing from them practical organisational models. From the evidence advanced by the author it seems probable that the models developed by and for Riverside may have wider applicability in the voluntary sector, especially for agencies which start with a self-help ethos but grow rapidly.

P. Bird and P. Morgan-Jones, *Financial Reporting by Charities*, Institute of Chartered Accountants in England and Wales, 1981.

This book reports a survey of charity accounts which sought to identify the reporting objectives of charities and the problems that arise in trying to fulfil them. The accounts of 85 charities were examined. The authors found substantial scope for improving reporting standards and ensuring consistent practices and comparability.

W. D. Birrell and A. W. Williamson, *Voluntary Organisations in the U.K. and Their Role in Combating Poverty*, New University of Ulster, Coleraine, 1980.

This is a short review of the voluntary sector role in the U.K. prepared for the Directorate General of Social Affairs of the Commission of European Communities.

W. E. Bjur, 'The International Manager and the Third Sector', *Public Administration Review*, September/October 1975, pp. 463–467.

Defining 'third sector management' as that area of management which occurs 'at the interface between public and private organisations', Bjur outlines some characteristic problem areas of third sector management.

Diverse entities have to be mobilised to consensus and concerted action. But the third sector organisation has to function in a politicised context which may not permit concerted action. Different clients and publics may apply different, ambiguous and ephemeral criteria to the evaluation of the organisation's effectiveness.

Lastly, there is the problem of multiple goals, identified by *Frank*. Multiple goals within an organisation may be accompanied by multiple policy-making points, conflicting and multiple standards and forced flexibility. As a consequence, system organisation may be impossible, and many people may feel insecure or threatened.

Although this article deals with the whole of the third sector and does not address itself to the particular problems of voluntary organisations, the problem areas it identifies coincide with suggestions made by writers on voluntary organisations in Britain. (See, for example, *Hadley et al, 1975*; *Handy, 1981*; *Leat et al, 1981* and *Wolfenden*.)

D. Borst and P. Montana (eds), *Managing Non-Profit Organisations*, AMACOM, New York. (ILL)

Borst and Montana have collected together in this book a number of articles which discuss the application to non-profit organisations in the USA of various management techniques originally developed for use by commercial organisations. Their aim is to make non-profit organisations more management conscious.

In Part One, 'Managing the Non-Profit Organisation – Can it be done?', some of the distinctive features and difficulties of management in the non-profit sector are discussed. Part Two discusses the systems approach to planning and analysis. Part Three includes articles about management by objectives, and Part Four is about project management and participatory management.

E. L. Brilliant, 'Private or Public: A Model of Ambiguities', *Social Service Review*, **47, 1973, pp. 384–396.**

This article discusses some issues raised by what the author regards as the 'blurring of formal boundaries between the private and the public' in modern government.

Brilliant argues that the sharing of public authority between government and voluntary institutions and the growth of 'federalism by contract' has produced a new model of society. This is a 'society of ambiguities' characterised by dissatisfaction with government, a crisis of authority caused by the evident fallibility of pluralism, and an inseparable link between social and economic policies.

M. Bruce, G. Darvill, S. Duncan, M. Rankin and M. Thompson, *Creative Partnership: A Study in Leicestershire of Voluntary Community Involvement*, **Volunteer Centre, 1976.**

This is a review of activities in Leicestershire involving neighbourhood care, residential care and volunteers working with statutory and voluntary agencies.

J. Burns, 'Social Workers Employed by Voluntary Agencies', *Social Work Today*, **9 May 1978, p. 11.**

This article lists examples that have come to the notice of the British Association of Social Workers (BASW) of unsatisfactory terms and conditions for social workers employed in voluntary agencies. These include having no trade union representatives, no disciplinary procedures, and no clear lines of communication between a lay committee and professional workers. The author suggests that 'salaries and conditions of service in many voluntary agencies are abysmal', with poor redundancy and pension entitlements, low salaries and 'partial' treatment of staff.

H. Butcher, P. Collis, A. Glen and P. Sills, *Community Groups in Action: Case Studies and Analysis*, **Routledge and Kegan Paul, 1980.**

The original aim of the study described in this book was to find appropriate methods of evaluating the effectiveness of community work interventions with local groups. But the researchers say that they realised at an early stage that the structure, dynamics, resources and goals of the groups were important in their own right.

The methodological approach, described in detail in the book, was to obtain a variety of first-hand evidence on the development of five community action

24

groups using a common checklist of factors relevant to the dynamics of organisation. A comparison of data eventually provided some concepts and analytical tools from which a series of propositions and hypotheses were drawn.

The propositions developed by the researchers relate to the role of community workers, the strategy and resources of groups, the organisation and goals of groups, and the relationship between groups and their environment. They suggest, for example, that a 'firm and appropriate structural framework' is a necessity for community groups. They also present some models of different ways in which community groups may interact with the beneficiaries and resource providers who constitute their environment.

H. Butcher: see also p. 92. see also p. 92.

R. M. L. Carruthers: see p. 37. see p. 37.

F. S. Chapin and J. E. Tsouderos, 'The Formalization Process in Voluntary Associations', *Social Forces*, **34, May 1956, pp. 342–344.** HM1

The authors studied 91 voluntary associations to examine their hypothesis that there is a 'cumulative process of formalization' in voluntary associations. This process was not precisely defined but was taken to imply 'a sequential, stage-by-stage development of voluntary associations over time; an increasing complexity in the social structure, a progressive prescription and standardization of social relationships and finally, an increasing bureaucratization of organization'.

The authors found that as membership of voluntary associations increased, the percentage of members attending meetings or volunteering for administrative tasks was smaller. As membership and the number of paid employees grew, board meetings became less frequent but the hours devoted to the association by executive officers increased. The formalisation process was in some respects discontinuous. For example, as membership increased, the frequency of general meetings first rose sharply and then decreased; reports to members first became more formal and less frequent and then increased in frequency although in a more formalised way; executive officers tended to first stay in power longer and then less long.

Chapin and Tsouderos conclude that formalisation in voluntary associations coincides with the growth of membership and 'is a general uniform process'. As 'one component or variable part of the organization develops and differentiates, the other elements are likewise developed and differentiated'. Although the speed of formalisation varies, it seems to occur irrespective of an association's goals.

Despite the fact that almost 30 years have passed since the publication of this paper, it remains a major contribution to the understanding of the process of *growth* in the voluntary sector. More recent writers, for example *Hyman* and *Jerman*, have gone beyond descriptions of growth and have addressed the practical issues such as whether formalisation can be checked and the impact of growth on those receiving services.

J. W. Chapman: see p. 80.

V. Chapman: see p. 31.

Charity

A monthly journal, first published in November 1983, concerned with the administration of charitable funds. It is published by the Charities Aid Foundation.

M. Chesterman, *Charities, Trusts and Social Welfare*, Weidenfeld and Nicolson, 1979.

This book describes the background history and the law relating to charitable welfare agencies.

T. N. Choille: see p. 40.

P. Collis: see p. 24 and p. 92.

***Community Care*, 'Voluntary Bodies, Past, Present and Future', Special Issue of *Community Care*, 5 April 1978.**

This is a collection of personal accounts and viewpoints on voluntary agencies and volunteering.

T. D. Connors (ed), *The Non-Profit Organization Handbook*, McGraw Hill, New York, 1980 (1). (ILL)

This book contains essays by different authors on various aspects of the non-profit sector in the United States.

An introductory chapter presents a typology according to purpose of non-profit organisations, using seventeen factors, and a chapter by David Horton Smith examines the possible impacts on society of the non-profit voluntary sector. There are also several essays included under the theme of 'leadership, management and control' of non-profit organisations, including one by *Connors* himself on 'Boards of Directors'.

T. D. Connors, 'The Boards of Directors' in T. D. Connors (ed), *The Non-Profit Organization Handbook*, McGraw Hill, New York, 1980 (2). (ILL)

This article concerns the governing bodies of non-profit organisations, which are known in the United States as 'Boards of Directors'.

After outlining the legal responsibilities of boards and recent trends in their composition, the author notes a tendency for boards to abdicate responsibilities for policy formulation to paid staff. He argues that the more staff an organisation has, the more its board should give more time to consideration of broad policy.

A board has the right to delegate its powers but must do so in an orderly way by 'carefully outlining which of its powers it wishes to delegate, to whom and with what reservations for how long'. It must also create 'the necessary executive structure and organisation to use effectively the delegated powers'.

True to the 'handbook' title of the book, Connors concludes his chapter with a checklist of characteristics of 'good' and 'effective' boards.

Although this article refers to boards of non-profit organisations generally and not just to those of voluntary agencies, the discussion it contains about powers and responsibilities is nevertheless very useful. The role of voluntary agency *governing bodies* and their relationship with paid staff can be ambiguous and problematic (see *Harris*, for example). By listing possible functions, responsibilities and good practice procedures, this article may be used to clarify some of these issues. (See also *Conrad and Glenn*.)

W. R. Conrad and W. E. Glenn, *The Effective Voluntary Board of Directors: What it is and how it works*, Swallow Press, Athens, Ohio, and London, 1983. (ILL)

The purpose of this book is 'to provide ground rules for effective boards' (that is, governing bodies), based on the authors' experience of teaching and consultancy work with the voluntary or 'third' sector.

The authors propose 'a basic management concept for voluntary organisations'. Management is concerned with four functions: service-delivery, resource development, personnel and business (the last three functions being support for service-delivery). All voluntary organisations, the authors argue, manage the same things, although *how* they do so is affected by their size and type. In each of the four functional areas, management activity is concerned with setting action goals and objectives and with target implementation, all within the broad framework of the organisation's overall policy or purposes.

Using this conceptual framework, the writers suggest the appropriate roles of boards and staff. Effective boards will concern themselves with the broad purposes of the organisation and with the goals and objectives aspects of management. Efficient staff will be primarily concerned with the 'implementation of targets' aspects of management.

The four management divisions are seen not only as an appropriate basis for staff organisation but also as a guide to committee structure. 'The standing committees of the board should correspond to the management divisions.' These committees should report directly to the board and not be 'screened' by an executive committee.

The only member of staff who is directly responsible to the board is the staff chief executive or paid director, and there must be 'a clear recognition, understanding and acceptance of the distinctive board and staff roles'. But there is also, and should be, a dynamic tension between board and staff which rests on mutual trust and need. What is sought is a 'dynamic, creative balance between professional dominance (which results in rubber-stamp boards) and lay dominance (which results in arrogation of the operational authority of the staff and eventual loss of purpose)'.

Despite the United States setting, this book addresses itself unequivocally to many of the main issues which arise in relation to voluntary sector *governing bodies*. The authors make practical suggestions for analysing and meeting the problems.

F. Courtney, 'Managing Charity? It can prove very difficult', *Local Government Chronicle*, 5 November 1982, pp. 1196–7.

This article is about the problems encountered by local authorities who are trustees of charities with outdated provisions and aims.

P. Cousins, 'Voluntary Organisations as Local Pressure Groups', *London Review of Public Administration*, 3, 1973, pp. 22–30.

This article reviews the literature on the role of voluntary organisations as pressure groups in local government.

P. Cousins, 'Voluntary Organisations and Local Government in Three South London Boroughs', *Public Administration*, 54, 1976, pp. 63–83.

This article describes a study in the London Boroughs of Bromley, Lambeth and Lewisham which investigated the extent to which local voluntary organisations were involved in local government decision-making.

P. Cousins, 'Participation and Pluralism in South London', *London Journal*, 4, 2, 1978, pp. 204–220.

Drawing on a study of three London boroughs (*Cousins*, 1976), this article attempts to classify relationships between local councils and local voluntary groups. Five types of relations are distinguished:

- close cooperation, in which members of voluntary organisations also sit as co-opted members on council committees
- dependency, in which voluntary organisations are dependent on the local authority for finance, staff or property, and are reluctant to criticise it
- conflict situation, in which, nevertheless, 'normal' channels of communication, such as tenants' associations, are used
- conflict situation, in which more extreme channels of communication, such as demonstrations and petitions, are used
- little contact between voluntary organisations and the local authority.

Cousins found that 'second order' (or intermediary) groups, such as Councils for Voluntary Service, were often 'almost local authority agents'. He also identified a 'grey area' of quasi-official bodies, such as tenants' consultative committees, which lie between voluntary organisations and council committees. Their members were frequently prominent members of several organisations and, therefore, useful in the local authority decision-making process.

The extent and nature of the role performed by local voluntary organisations in an area was mostly determined by what the local authority wanted them to do; but, on the other hand, council officers recognised their own need for the cooperation of voluntary organisations in providing services. Moreover, voluntary organisations were able to influence local authority policy.

The author concludes that there is pluralism in the local political process, in the sense that many groups are involved, but that local authorities are not dominated by voluntary agencies.

This article grapples with the important issue of the relationship with local authorities from a political science standpoint. Its conclusions may be contrasted with the work of U.S. authors who have approached a similar topic from the viewpoint of the voluntary agencies themselves; see, for example, *Berg and Wright*, *Hartogs and Weber*, *1978*, and *Kramer*, *1981*.

B. Crowe, *The Playgroup Movement*, Allen and Unwin, 1983.

This is a revised version of a report first written in 1973. It defines playgroups, examines their needs and problems, and traces their development.

J. Cullis and P. Jones, 'The Control of Private Charities: Some Evidence and Comments', *Public Administration*, 60, 3, 1982, pp. 356–363.

In this article the authors comment on an earlier article by *Marshall*.

29

T. Dartington, *Task Force*, Mitchell Beazley, 1971.

This book describes the early history of the voluntary agency for the elderly, 'Task Force', now renamed 'Pensioners' Link'.

T. Dartington, *Volunteers and Psychiatric Aftercare*, Volunteer Centre and MIND, 1978.

This booklet reports on the work in psychiatric aftercare of two local MIND associations. It focuses on the innovatory role of voluntary organisations and their relationships with statutory authorities.

G. Darvill, *Bargain or Barricade*, Volunteer Centre, 1975.

This booklet discusses the role of local authority Social Services Departments, in meeting social need through involving the 'community', i.e. volunteers.

G. Darvill: see also p. 24 and p. 68.

B. Davies, *The Cost Effectiveness Imperative: Social Services and Volunteers*, Occasional Paper, Volunteer Centre, 1980.

This paper argues that more effort should be made to seek contexts in which formal social services and communal forms of social organisation are combined and made mutually supporting.

R. Davies: see p. 14.

L. Day: see p. 106.

N. Deakin, 'Providing an Ambulance Wagon is not what we're here for', *Voluntary Action*, Autumn, 1982, pp. 16–17.

This article is adapted from the Nancy Fear Memorial Lecture delivered at the AGM of the Birmingham Settlement in May, 1982. It argues that central government is encouraging the voluntary sector to do what it does worst; that is, to imitate local and central government bureaucracies. The strength of the sector, it is argued, lies in its flexibility, and in its innovative and critical abilities.

J. Dearlove, *The Politics of Policy in Local Government*, Cambridge Univeristy Press, 1973.

This book is an examination of local policy-making processes in a London borough. It includes an examination of the contribution to local policy made by local voluntary groups.

Department of Health and Social Security Library, *Bibliography B132*, **DHSS, 1980.**

This pamphlet contains selected references, with abstracts, on the role of voluntary agencies in personal social services provision.

Department of Health and Social Security Library, *Bibliography B133*, **DHSS, 1983.**

This pamphlet lists references, with abstracts, on self-help groups.

R. Dewar: see p. 44.

M. Dockray: see p. 70.

D. Donnison with V. Chapman, M. Meacher, A. Sears and K. Urwin, *Social Policy and Administration Revisited*, **Allen and Unwin, 1975.**

This is a revised and updated version of a book first published in 1965. It comprises a number of case studies designed to throw some light on the question 'Why and how do innovations in social policy come about?' An introductory chapter discusses the nature of social administration as a field of study and a concluding chapter draws out from the case studies some ideas about the nature of social policy change and innovation.

Although most of the case studies focus on aspects of statutory, or public, welfare service provision, two concern voluntary agencies. One, entitled 'Crisis in a Canadian Service for Children', describes conflicts which arose in an agency when new initiatives by staff could not be sustained by available finances. Clarification of the agency's aims and methods eventually emerged in the course of a struggle for power in which not only the staff and governing body, but also important groups and individuals in the local community, were involved. The authors conclude that 'the surprising thing is not that the Children's Aid Society ran into trouble, but that any organisation whose services are unrealistically subdivided, inspected and controlled by one body, financed by half a dozen, subject to arbitration by several, directed by a self-selected Board and forced to rely for the money to support an important part of its work, on fluctuating voluntary contributions, should normally have functioned so smoothly and effectively'.

A second case study traces the evolution of procedures for the improvement of professional skills and working methods in a local office of the Family Welfare Association (FWA). As in the Canadian case study, innovations initiated by staff had resource implications which, in turn, provoked internal conflicts and revealed divergent expectations among those involved in running the agency. The agency's administrative structure, in particular its uncertainty about the relative power of the central office and local groups, was ill-adapted for resolving these conflicts. Thus, the authors found that 'the most striking thing about the FWA's attempts to reorganise itself was the cycle – repeated every two or three years – of crisis, reappraisal, discussion, minor modification and crisis'.

Concluding comments at the end of each case study and a final concluding chapter of the book draw on all the case studies without necessarily distinguishing between voluntary and statutory agencies.

This is one of the few substantial studies which includes both voluntary and statutory welfare agencies. It thus provides an opportunity to examine the extent to which voluntary agencies have distinctive characteristics. Difficulties involved in securing financial and other support for innovatory initiatives, and the lack of structures and processes within voluntary agencies to facilitate conflict resolution, emerge as problems which are especially likely to arise in the voluntary sector.

Another study of the governing structure of the FWA is found in *Lenn, 1972*.

J. Douglas, *Why Charity? The Case for a Third Sector*, Sage Publications, Beverley Hills, California, and London, 1983.

This book attempts to provide a rationale for the existence of 'third sector' institutions in society and to distinguish the proper role of the sector in relation to government and commercial institutions.

S. Duncan: see p. 24.

K. Edwards, 'Collective Working in a Small Non-Statutory Organisation', *MDU Bulletin*, 3/4, July 1984, pp. 6–8.

This article describes the decision to 'go collective' in a local umbrella body working in the single homeless field. It describes the problems that arose and concludes with a list of twelve suggestions for anyone thinking of setting up a 'collective workplace'. These include paying close attention to job descriptions, decision-making processes, administrative tasks, relations with the management committee, pay structures and public relations.

S. Etherington, 'Community Wares in the Private Market', *Social Work Today*, 7 June 1983, pp. 6–7.

This article discusses the purchase of social work services by Social Services Departments, either in the private-sector market or from voluntary agencies. It queries whether voluntary sector provision is really cheaper in the long run and whether purchasing services outside the local authority can do much to encourage participatory democracy. (See also *Judge*.)

A. Etzioni, 'The Third Sector and Domestic Missions', *Public Administration Review*, July-August, 1973, pp. 314–323.

This article was one of the first to discuss the idea that social and economic needs may be met not only by the private and governmental sectors, but also by a 'third sector'. The 'third sector' provides a means of combining the best of both worlds; 'efficiency and expertise from the business world with public interest, accountability and broader planning from government'.

S. Evans: see p. 14.

C. Farrell: see p. 43.

W. Feek, *Management Committees – Practising Community Control*, National Youth Bureau, 1982 (1).

The aim of this booklet is to help youth and community groups to establish and support local management committees. Interviews with workers involved in committee work are presented to provide examples of techniques, strategies, and 'working models on which the basis and role of committees, committee members and support staff can be shaped'.

W. Feek, *The Way We Work – Making Staff Teams Effective*, National Youth Bureau, 1982 (2).

This booklet includes interviews with two 'non-hierarchical' staff teams in voluntary agencies.

W. Feek, *Who takes the strain? The Choices for Staff Support*, National Youth Bureau, 1982 (3).

This booklet discusses staff support systems, 'identifying issues and noting different approaches which some agencies have used'. The 'heart' of any staff support system is described as including job descriptions, supervision of work and performance appraisals. Intervention regarding the performance of staff may be directed towards support and/or control.

W. Feek, *Steps in Time: A Guide to Agency Planning*, National Youth Bureau, 1983.

The purpose of this booklet is 'to help people in youth and community work agencies recognise the value of good planning' and the importance of not acting in an *ad hoc*, unsystematic way in response to urgent problems. The focus is on how to determine which social needs and client groups the agency will respond to. Factors to be taken into account in making such decisions include the agency's philosophy and history, staff views, the management committee, the local community, the national situation, existing agency commitments and available resources.

F. Field, *Poverty and Politics: The Inside Story of the Child Poverty Action Group Campaigns in the 1970s*, Heinemann, 1982.

This book provides a history and background of CPAG campaigns. It discusses the 'poverty' and 'family' lobbies and pressure group activities.

R. Fizdale, 'The Voluntary Agency: Structure versus Accountability', *Social Casework*, October 1974, pp. 478–483.

The author of this article, who is the Executive Director of a voluntary agency, argues that the 'industrial model' in which boards take all programme decisions and represent the donor community, while staff offer services as paid employees of boards, is outdated. Voluntary social services must now be accountable to their community. They must accept the implications of multiple funding sources and the receipt of public funds; and they must adapt to the professionalism of their staff who are well able to judge the needs of their clients.

A review of organisational structures is required to mirror these changes. A collaborative relationship between staff and boards, it is argued, 'offers a more logical system for today's voluntary agency's accountability to its source of income, its clients and the profession of social work'. A collaborative relationship means that both board and staff are 'equally invested in the provision of a needed community service and are equally accountable for the quality of service provided and for its cost', even though they bring to the agency different assets and competence.

The main value of this article lies in the attempt, by a *practitioner*, to provide a theoretical underpinning for a familiar problem in voluntary agencies; that is, the relationship between governing bodies and paid staff. Fizdale's concept of equal

34

accountability may be contrasted with the standpoint of other authors who have preferred to look for distinctive functions and accountability. See, for example, *Conrad and Glenn*, and *Weber, 1975*.

A. G. Frank, 'Goal Ambiguity and Conflicting Standards: An Approach to the Study of Organisation', *Human Organization*, Winter, 1958–9, pp. 8–13.

This article proposes a new approach to the study of organisation – one based on an assumption that organisations have ambiguous goals which produce conflicting standards for members' behaviour. The idea, in turn, underpins a paper by *McGill and Wooten, 1975 (2)* on models of 'third sector' organisations.

A. Freedman: see p. 93.

A. Freedman: see p. 93.

P. Gay and J. P. Keathley, *Mobilising Voluntary Resources – the Work of the Voluntary Services Coordinator*, Kings Fund Centre, and Volunteer Centre, 1982.

This book describes a study of the work of 'voluntary service co-ordinators'; people in statutory or voluntary agencies who as part of their routine activity regularly recruit and/or place those who deliver voluntary care.

D. Gerard, 'Foundations, Charity and the Financial Crisis', *Social Service Quarterly*, 49, 3, 1976, pp. 94–98.

This article discusses the implications of the 1976 inflationary crisis for the foundations which contribute to the funding of voluntary agencies. The author is concerned that foundations may be pressured to continue funding projects which are 'ripe for absorption into the statutory services' and that this will detract from the foundations' freedom to foster new initiatives or 'new and important programmes of marginal interest to governments'.

  The author suggests that a 'coherent priority-orientated approach' to funding by foundations would help to prevent such a trend towards unrealistic expectations.

D. Gerard, *Charities in Britain: Conservatism or Change?*, Bedford Square Press/NCVO, 1983.

This book is a summary report of a study entitled 'Charity and Change: A Profile of the Voluntary Sector', also published by Bedford Square Press/NCVO and available only on microfiche.

  The core of the study was provided by the results of two surveys. One was conducted through a postal questionnaire by Gallup Poll and investigated the views of 298 chief executives of U.K. charities about organisational aspects of their charities. The other study was a major survey of moral and social values in Europe by the European Value Systems Study Group (EVSSG); it was concerned with volunteers, public perceptions of charity and the characteristics of beneficiaries.

Drawing selectively on these two studies as well as on other publications, the author provides a profile of the voluntary sector; an exposition of its underlying norms, its legal framework, its range of activities and its organisational and management characteristics.

Looking at the relationship between management style and organisation structure, the author distinguishes three different approaches: 'a hierarchical authoritarian approach; a consultative approach with considerable delegation of powers; and a fully participative approach'. He suggests that the organisational form chosen is often related to a charity's broad attitude towards order and change. 'A hierarchical form of organisation is correlated with a conservative view-of-society and with the religious, compassionate and service-oriented philosophy-of-operation indicative of beneficence. A participative form is associated with a progressive view-of-society and with the social and political values indicative of solidarity.'

A section of the book on 'Management and Effectiveness' points out some characteristics of voluntary agencies which, though not unique, require special consideration when searching for management techniques appropriate to the voluntary sector. These include the value-based nature of their work; trusteeship; volunteer workers; lack of security and career structures for paid staff; lack of client feedback; and the need for accountability to external funders. Using survey and other data, the author then presents a picture of the most frequent management problems and issues in the voluntary sector. These include designing an organisational structure which meets the wishes of staff and sponsors but is also an effective medium for executing the agency's policies; a structure which is 'relevant to both the creative/innovative/professional aspects of the work and the more routine/structural/measurable components of the task'.

The author's consultations with practitioners in the voluntary sector suggested that their dominant management problems were in the areas of manpower, communication and internal dynamics, followed closely by industrial relations, volunteers and strategic problems. The Gallup survey largely confirmed this picture.

A final chapter of the book discusses the implications of the study for three aspects of management education in the voluntary sector: for consultancy on specific problems in specific organisations; for the management education of individuals; and for the development of advisory, support, and referral services for the voluntary sector as a whole.

In presenting and examining some empirical data about the organisation and management of voluntary agencies, the author has made an important contribution to the U.K. literature in this field. Assumptions about the vibrancy, flexibility and effectiveness of the voluntary sector can be examined more critically in the light of these findings. As the author himself suggests, his work can help government and funders to be clear about the nature, relative importance and representativeness of the agencies with which they are dealing. The book also provides an opportunity for the voluntary sector itself to reflect upon its effectiveness.

D. Gerard, L. Taylor-Harrington and R. M. L. Carruthers, *Management and Effectiveness in the Voluntary Sector: Inter-Charity Comparisons as a Management Tool*, Centre for Interfirm Comparison, 1981.

This booklet provides a case study of the adaptation for the voluntary sector of a management technique developed originally for the commercial sector. The aim of the technique is to help improve the operational effectiveness of voluntary bodies through making and using systematic comparisons between similar kinds of organisation.

F. Gladstone, *Voluntary Action in a Changing World*, Bedford Square Press/NCVO, 1979.

This book reviews the record of the welfare state and argues for a change of approach, towards welfare pluralism and more voluntary action. (See also *Hadley and Hatch, 1981* and *Webb, 1981*.)

F. Gladstone, *Charity Law and Social Justice*, Bedford Square Press/ NCVO, 1982 (1).

This book describes the background to current laws relating to charities and assesses the need for their reform.

F. Gladstone, 'Political Activity: How far can Charities Go?', *Voluntary Action*, Autumn 1982, pp. 13–14 (2).

This article, which draws on the author's report 'Charity Law and Social Justice' (*Gladstone*, 1982 (1)), puts forward some ideas for changing the laws which at present regulate and curtail charities' political activities.

W. A. Glaser and D. L. Sills (eds), *The Government of Associations*, Bedminster Press, Totowa, New Jersey, 1966. (ILL)

This book provides 47 selections from books, journals and research reports in the behavioural sciences on the general theme of running associations. Most of the selections are reports of empirical research and not directives for action. However, the material is grouped together and introduced by the editors in such a way as to guide the reader who seeks more practical, prescriptive material 'from one selection to another and to point out possible applications to a situation he might face'.

The resulting volume, although now old, provides an invaluable source book for both students and leaders of voluntary agencies. It covers not only material directly concerned with running voluntary agencies, but also a representative selection of general sociological and organisational literature which can be applied to the voluntary association setting. (Several items are noted individually in this bibliography.)

A. Glen: see p. 24 and p. 92.

W. E. Glen: see p. 27.

E. M. Goldberg and others, *Monitoring Voluntary Action*, ARVAC, 1983.

This booklet arose from a seminar organised in July 1982 by the Association of Researchers into Voluntary Action. It comprises papers by several authors.

An opening paper by E. M. Goldberg provides a general discussion of the issues raised by evaluation of social care and concludes that evaluation of work done with community groups may be more difficult than evaluating individual client care work. Other papers provide case studies of attempts to evaluate the work of particular projects which used, or are using, volunteers.

Goodman Committee, *Charity Law and Voluntary Organisations*, Bedford Square Press/NCVO, 1976.

This is the report of an independent committee of inquiry into the law relating to charitable activities, set up by the National Council of Social Service (NCSS, now NCVO) and chaired by Lord Goodman.

M. Goodman: see p. 82.

C. W. Gordon and N. Babchuk, 'A Typology of Voluntary Associations' in W. A. Glaser and D. L. Sills (eds), *The Government of Associations*, Bedminster Press, Totowa, New Jersey, 1966. Reprinted from the *American Sociological Review*, 24, 2, February 1959, pp. 22–29.

This article presents a typology of voluntary associations based on three 'dimensions' used in sociological thinking:

- whether membership is open or restricted (accessibility)
- whether membership confers social prestige on members (status-defining capacity)

38

- the functions that an association performs for members (instrumental, expressive or both).

The authors suggest that their typology can be used to generate hypotheses for research.

A. Gouldner, 'The Secrets of Organizations', in R. Kramer and H. Specht (eds), *Readings in Community Organization Practice*, Prentice Hall, Englewood Cliffs, New Jersey, 1969.

This article points out some of the discrepancies between the theory and practice of running welfare agencies.

As regards governing bodies, Gouldner argues that there is a 'nominal assumption' that the board of a welfare agency 'serves to communicate to the staff and to the executive what are the larger community problems and interests' and that staff pursue goals indicated by the board. A 'secret' fact however, is that it is, the staff who often exercise control and, in many agencies, the board serves to legitimate the staff's conception of community needs and priorities.

Another 'secret' in many welfare agencies is the way in which, rather than the board hiring staff, the staff in effect hire the board.

Gouldner seeks to explain these observations and suggests that what is involved is yet another 'secret' – an 'exchange' between agency staff and influential persons in the local community. These latter, by serving on boards, open resources to agencies and symbolise their legitimacy. In exchange, the agency gives the civic-minded citizen an opportunity for public visibility and status achievement.

In bringing to public attention the real power relationships between *governing bodies and staff*, this paper, despite its age, makes a highly pertinent contribution. Later writers have drawn attention to the same phenomenon. (See, for example, *Hartogs and Weber, 1974, Senor*, and *Harris*.)

H. Griffiths, *The Development of Local Voluntary Action*: *An interpretative account of a conference held at Swanwick, Derbyshire, 23–25 January 1981*, Volunteer Centre, 1981.

The conference reported and discussed in this booklet was a part of the Home Office Voluntary Services Unit's programme to foster the development of local voluntary action.

In the earlier chapters, Griffiths discusses the nature of voluntary work and voluntary organisations and then reviews the experiences described in the conference case studies. He argues that the studies illustrate the need to encourage and support volunteers and to recognise that they are more often discovered though personal contacts than through formal recruitment and selection. The studies also show the importance of both vertical relationships between national and local bodies and horizontal relationships between voluntary associations and other community institutions.

Griffiths goes on to explore the weaknesses of voluntary action, including poor accountability and the obstacles presented by government policies and structures. He concludes that the development of local voluntary action demands re-thinking about concepts of representative democracy, formal administration and professional exclusiveness.

The final chapter of the book comprises the case studies, descriptions of their own projects by conference participants. Some of the descriptions are impressionistic and anecdotal, while others attempt to be more analytical. An account of the Forest Hill Advice Centre, for example, suggests guidelines for success in developing local voluntary action.

Whilst this booklet does not address itself to the details of organising and managing voluntary organisations, as a personal account of an exploratory debate it succeeds well in drawing on individual experiences to clarify some of the major problems in developing local voluntary action. The need for care in such matters as involving volunteers, relationships with Social Services Departments and choosing goals, emerges clearly.

H. Griffiths, T. N. Choille and J. Robinson, *Yesterday's Heritage or Tomorrow's Resource: A Study of Voluntary Organizations Providing Social Services in Northern Ireland*, Occasional Papers in Social Administration, New University of Ulster, Coleraine, 1978.

The study reported in this booklet focused on voluntary organisations providing social services in Northern Ireland. 700 organisations were initially located and 479 provided preliminary information about themselves. In 70 agencies detailed interviews were conducted with a senior member of staff about origin and aims; human and financial resources; structure and system of management; area of welfare intervention and relationship with the statutory sector and other voluntary agencies.

Half the organisations surveyed had been started by individuals and the continued presence of founders often created special difficulties of regeneration and change. In their structure, most agencies conformed to a familiar patttern; that is, a loosely defined open membership which only met annually and allowed the governing body (a self-perpetuating elite) to retain firm control of the organisation. Volunteers and donors were excluded from policy-making although paid staff had some marginal influence.

The majority of volunteers were employed by a majority of large organisations and were mostly used in direct service provision. Most paid staff, however, were employed for administrative and support tasks.

The authors conclude that the strength of the voluntary sector lies in its ability to meet need through individual personal relationships and that the time of its paid and unpaid staff are a unique resource. However, its strength is also a weakness. A voluntary agency is by nature and instinct unable to give much consideration to the development of the voluntary sector as a whole. Also it tends to concentrate on the mechanics of providing a service rather than on assessing the true extent of need which exists and then attempting to discover if the voluntary contribution can be enlarged to meet it.

On the basis of their empirical material, the authors have been able to make some useful suggestions about the *distinctive features* of voluntary welfare-service agencies.

Their conclusions about the power of governing bodies contrast with the views of other authors (e.g. *Gouldner*, *Senor*) who have argued that staff tend to be relatively dominant. The doubts raised about agencies' ability to seek out and respond to new needs echoes the arguments of *Kramer*, *1979 (1)*. but contrasts with the views of those authors who regard flexibility and responsiveness as distinguishing features of the voluntary sector (for example, *Hadley and Hatch*, *1981*).

R. Guiton, *Voluntary Organisation – Some Effects of Local Government Reforms*, Occasional Paper, NCSS (now Bedford Square Press/NCVO), 1967.

This document describes the impact on Councils of Social Services (CSSs, now Councils of Voluntary Service or CVSs), of the local government reorganisations of the 1960s.

J. R. Gusfield, 'The Woman's Christian Temperance Union', in A. W. Glaser and D. L. Sills (eds), *The Government of Associations*, Bedminster Press, Totowa, New Jersey, 1966. (ILL). See also J. R. Gusfield, 'The Problem of Generations in an Organizational Structure', *Social Forces*, 35, 4, May 1957, pp. 323–330.

These articles provide a case study of a voluntary association which failed to adapt quickly to changes in its environment (the repeal of Prohibition). An entrenched oligarchy was able to ignore grass-roots revolts, and thus the organisation declined.

D. Guthrie, 'The Place of Voluntary Organisations in Great Britain', *Journal of the Royal College of Physicians of London*, 13, 4, 1979, pp. 237–238.

This article argues that voluntary organisations are an essential part of the welfare state. They must be efficient and complementary to statutory services. Volunteers must be controlled by professionals and should be used as an 'extra pair of hands'.

Hackney Community Action (HCA), *Community Groups Information Pack*, 1983.

This booklet is a guide 'intended to help individuals and groups who are applying for money for the first time and management committee members and paid workers of established groups'. There are chapters on grants, legal aspects of employing workers, premises and insurance. A chapter on management committees discusses not only the skills of running and contributing to meetings but also the composition of the committee and its responsibilities.

R. Hadley and S. Hatch, *Research on the Voluntary Sector*, Social Science Research Council (SSRC), London, 1980.

This is a brief report, prepared for the Sociology and Administration Committee of the Social Science Research Council, of two workshops held by the authors for SSRC. The aim was to assist the allocation of the Committee's budget for voluntary sector work.

The authors describe the report as presenting 'proposals for exploring alternative patterns of welfare provision'. They suggest that there are three main levels for analysis of the voluntary sector: the individual involved in voluntary action; the relationship between the voluntary and statutory sectors; and organisations. The authors' list of aspects of organisations in which research is needed includes origins, geographical distribution, membership, achievements, funding, and accountability.

R. Hadley and S. Hatch, *Social Welfare and the Failure of the State*, Allen and Unwin, 1981.

The central focus of this book is the role of the state in the provision of social welfare services and the possible alternatives.

The authors provide a critique of the expansion of centralised statutory services, arguing that they have had little effect on inequalities and are unresponsive to the intended beneficiaries. The advantages and limitations of alternative sources of care – the informal, voluntary and commercial sectors – are examined. It is then suggested that a pluralist, participative and decentralised pattern of services is required which can maximise the contribution of the informal and voluntary sectors within a framework of priorities and standards set by the statutory sector.

Some of the efforts already made to achieve decentralisation and public involvement in social provision are referred to, including lay involvement in statutory community care services and patch teams in local authority social services departments. Bureaucratic and participatory systems of social services organisation are contrasted with regard to factors such as authority sources, organisational structure, mode of decision-making, staff roles, user roles and forms of accountability. The main organisational characteristics of community-centred patches are contrasted with those of traditional client-centred area teams.

This book concentrates on the dysfunctions of the statutory sector; the voluntary sector is given much less thorough examination. The assumption appears to be made that voluntary agencies delivering welfare services may be able to avoid problems such as unresponsiveness, formalisation and inflexibility. However, as discussed in the Introduction to this bibliography, there can be little doubt that the voluntary sector is not immune to these and other organisational problems. (See, for example, *Gerard, 1983*; *Handy, 1981*; *Webb, 1981*; and *Wolfenden*.)

R. Hadley, A. Webb and C. Farrell, *Across the Generations: Old People and Young Volunteers*, Allen and Unwin, 1975.

This book is an evaluative account of the work of Task Force. At the time when the study began in 1970, the aims of the agency were to organise the work of young volunteers with the elderly, to educate young volunteers about social problems, and to encourage community action. The study was conducted in four London boroughs and sought to establish, through surveys of people involved and observation of the agency, the nature of clients' needs, the characteristics of volunteers, the quality and quantity of service provided by volunteers, and variables likely to affect these factors.

The authors find that the organisational processes of Task Force could have been used to reduce the risk of failure and improve the success rate in relationships between volunteers and the elderly. The agency's employed staff could have played a more significant clearing house role in the selection, assessment, allocation and support of volunteers. The more informal methods used were not suitable for a sizeable voluntary organisation with large caseloads. However, at the time of the study there was confusion within the agency about which of the agency's aims should be given priority and managers were giving relatively low priority to improving and maintaining the clearing house function, emphasising, instead, its educational and community goals. However, the effect of the original founder's views, as well as pressure from local authority funders, was to emphasise quantity rather than quality in Task Force work.

Three possible models of organising a volunteer visiting programme are proposed and their organisational implications are discussed. The extensive service model reflects Task Force's original intentions, but it may produce an uneven and a poor quality service. The number of unsuccessful relationships in this model could however be reduced by restricting volunteers' activities to those requiring little supervision and by concentrating the agency's resources on selection procedures. An alternative intensive approach would concentrate on issues of quality, emphasising need identification, and the assessment and support of volunteers. Employed staff would require some social work skills. This model implies smaller numbers of volunteers and elderly visited. A third model, the composite approach, would pursue high quality intensive work while using volunteers as extensively as possible for both visiting and management functions. Volunteers would have a career pattern from extensive to intensive visiting and to staff-support work. Staff would be more specialised and skilled. Because the model implies an increased degree of central control over local groups for policy and monitoring, it raises a dilemma for an agency committed to minimal 'bureaucracy'.

Although it was not the prime purpose of the study, this book provides a useful insight into the problems which can beset a voluntary agency in rapid *growth*. The study also provides insight into more general organisational issues for voluntary agencies including the management and control of volunteers and the compatibility of service-providing goals with other goals. Chapter 9, which discusses three models of *organising volunteers*, is particularly helpful in illustrating the differing organisational and management implications of policy choices in voluntary agencies. (See also *Shenfield and Allen*.)

J. Hage and R. DeWar, 'Elite Values Versus Organizational Structure in Predicting Innovation', *Administrative Science Quarterly*, **18, 3, 1973, pp. 279–290.**

Research concerned with the prediction of organisational performance and change has tended to concentrate on structural variables (such as complexity, centralisation and formalisation) as predictors. The authors of this paper aimed to redress the balance by examining values (of leaders, elites and members) as predictors of change and innovation. They studied sixteen health and welfare agencies in a large mid-western city.

They found that value explanations were better predictors of change than structural ones and that the values of the elite inner circle were 'more important than those of the executive director or of the entire staff in predicting innovation'.

Among the structural variables, the strongest predictor of change was complexity. But elite values were slightly stronger predictors than complexity. The authors argue from this finding that 'elites are not totally determined by the kind of organisation they lead, but are able to manipulate their organisations, at least for innovation'.

D. C. Hague: see p. 92.

Handy Working Party Report, *Improving Effectiveness in Voluntary Organisations*, **Bedford Square Press/NCVO, 1981.**

This booklet is the final report of a working party which was invited in 1980 by NCVO to consider how voluntary organisations might be assisted to maintain and improve their effectiveness over the coming decade. The main source of information for the working party was a 1978 Gallup survey on management in the voluntary sector and comments sent in by 'a wide range of organisations and individuals involved in the voluntary sector'.

The authors identified two levels of management problems in voluntary organisations. The first-level problems consisted of 'admitted' or 'presenting' problems. The Gallup survey asked directors of voluntary organisations for the three most serious management problems facing their organisation excluding finance. The most frequently mentioned problems were staff shortage, accommodation, educating public opinion, recruitment and staff turnover, and development problems. The working party found that other important, first-level problems in voluntary agencies included leadership style, change, resource allocation and relationships with the organisational environment.

The working party thought that a second set of problems which were less readily talked about lay behind the first-level problems. They concerned areas such as values, relationships, goals, decisions and people. Even where first-level problems were resolved, the second-level ones often remained. There are no right answers; each organisation has to find its own answers and these may change over time; for they are 'to do with an organisation's chosen identity, purposes and style'.

The authors suggest that the problems may be matched by courses, services and mutual support. Courses and services 'relate more directly to the first-level problems'. 'The second-level problems can best be helped by more systems of mutual support.' It is stressed that individuals who follow courses or use services should be helped and encouraged to follow-up the fruits of their learning within their organisation by moving on to tackle second-level problems.

The report concludes with a recommendation that NCVO should establish 'a small brokerage function' to foster and maintain different ways of helping and supporting the search by voluntary organisations for improved managerial effectiveness.

This Report represents the first attempt in the U.K. to address the specific *problems of organisation* in the voluntary sector. It has the considerable merits of clarity and brevity and its main recommendation – the establishment of a management development unit by the NCVO – has already been implemented.

C. Handy, 'Organisations in Search of a Theory', *MDU Bulletin* I, May 1983, p. 8 (1).

This article argues that it would be a tragedy if, because of distaste for traditional models of management, the voluntary sector turns its back on emerging rules and principles about the running of their sorts of organisation. This 'emerging theory' is one that views 'organisations as networks rather than machines, as sets of coalitions and alliances rather than departments'.

In developing further a theory of governance or management for voluntary agencies, it may be possible to apply some ideas from wider political systems such as democracy, separation of the executive from policy-making, accountability and federalism.

Some comments on Handy's arguments appear in C. Coverdale and R. Gordon, 'The Search for a Theory: Some Unexpected Signposts', *MDU Bulletin* 3/4, July 1984, p. 16.

C. Handy, 'Management in an Artists' Colony', *Marriage Guidance*, Summer, 1983 (2), pp. 10–13.

This edited version of a speech given to the AGM of the National Marriage Guidance Council lists the questions which an effective voluntary agency will ask about itself. It should consider its policy-making machinery, its criteria for success and the kind of organisation it is, i.e. feudal, bureaucratic, or professional.

M. E. Harris, *Governing Bodies in Voluntary Agencies: A Study of Local Management Committees in the Citizens Advice Bureaux Service*, M.A. Dissertation, Brunel University, 1983.

This study of local management committees in the CAB service was intended to shed light on the role of governing bodies in voluntary agencies. Fourteen unstructured interviews were conducted with people holding various positions within the CAB service in order to achieve a range of perceptions about the role of management committees in theory and practice.

Five main functional areas were found to be allocated to management committees in the agency's official statements: securing resources; selecting and appointing paid and voluntary staff; carrying the legal responsibilities of charity trustees and employers; representing CAB to the local community and the community to CAB; and involvement in agency policy-making at the national level.

People interviewed in the study thought management committees mostly took their legal and resource-raising functions seriously but regarded them as no more than 'a formality'. With respect to staffing matters, they seemed to be 'casual' and were often lacking in the necessary expertise. The representative functions were more usually carried out, if at all, by bureau staff rather than by management committees. Involvement in policy-making was limited to being 'put in the picture' by bureau organisers.

The author suggests that a 'self-fulfilling cycle of expectations' was established between management committees and bureau organisers, such that staff did not expect to share problems and decisions with their committees. Committees, in their turn, did not see any need to encourage staff to do so. The existence of a national headquarters staff, high regard for volunteers, and infrequent committee meetings were among the factors that reinforced the cycle.

The author raises issues about the role of local governing bodies in national voluntary agencies. For example, if management committees were less passive, would staff benefit by having fewer administrative burdens and more psychological support? Would the agency's clients benefit if governors took more interest in monitoring the quality of service provided and in clarifying accountability for work done by volunteer and other staff? What is the appropriate role of local

46

governing bodies within an agency with a strong national headquarters and public face?

The study concludes with a presentation of some alternative models of how management committees might function in a voluntary agency like the CAB service.

This study addresses itself to a subject which has received more attention in the United States than in Britain, despite the fact that the role of governing bodies raises major problems. The particular value of this work lies in the attempt not only to describe the difficulties of the governing body-staff relationship; but also to develop an explanation.

A brief summary of some parts of this dissertation is found in: M. Harris, 'Management Committees in Voluntary Agencies', in B. Knight (ed), *Management in Voluntary Organisations*, Occasional Paper No. 6, ARVAC, 1984.

N. Hartogs and J. Weber, *Boards of Directors, A Study of Current Practices in Board Management and Board Operations in Voluntary Hospitals, Health and Welfare Organisations*, Oceana Publications, New York, 1974. (ILL)

This is the report of a study which sought 'reliable, representative, quantified data' about current practices in the operation of governing bodies ('Boards') of voluntary welfare agencies. The objectives of the study were to stimulate critical examination of management in voluntary agencies; provide a means of comparison between organisations; and facilitate the development of guidelines and training material for voluntary agencies.

Information was provided by a self-selected sample of Board members, Board Presidents (usually called Chairmen in Britain) and paid Executive Directors of 296 voluntary organisations in the Greater New York area.

As regards the membership of Boards, men outnumbered women in the ratio 2:1; the majority were in the 25–65 years age range and the most usual employment backgrounds were banking, law or business. New members were usually the result of active recruitment, often by existing Board members. Frequently, they had had some previous contact with the organisation, either as a volunteer or as a client. Informants agreed that the main functions of Boards included policy-making, fund-raising, committee work and recruitment of Board members. Presidents and Executive Directors would have liked Board members to take a more active role in training members and in 'interpreting the organisation's work to the community'. The Executive Directors mostly regarded themselves as consultants to Boards, and Board members agreed with this view. Board Presidents looked on their Executive Directors as equal partners.

Several problems uncovered by this study's informants included getting inactive Board members to participate more; recruiting younger Board members; obtaining more funding from charitable foundations; establishing priorities; and making agencies' programmes more relevant to changing needs.

This is an important, wide-ranging descriptive study which illuminates the position of governing bodies in U.S. voluntary agencies. The view it presents of a relatively active and self-aware governing body may be contrasted with the view of other authors who have suggested that paid staff have a more dominant role. (See, for example, *Gouldner*, *Senor* and *Harris*.)

N. Hartogs and J. Weber, *Impact of Government Funding on the Management of Voluntary Agencies*, Greater New York Fund/United Way, New York, 1978. (ILL)

This book reports a study of 148 voluntary agencies which come under the umbrella of the Greater New York Fund, an intermediary body which distributes funds to voluntary agencies. The aim of the study was to investigate the effect on voluntary social service agencies of receiving government funding.

Government funding was not found to threaten 'voluntarism'; in fact, the government and voluntary sectors were found to be complementing each other's work and government funding was encouraging the survival of agencies. Nor was there any evidence of agencies' core programmes being displaced, although adjustments to programmes had to be made sometimes to conform with government requirements. Some agencies however, did experience problems in meeting government accountability regulations and in managing the funds made available to them.

The authors conclude that government funds, in themselves, are not a threat to voluntary agencies but that the effective management of those funds may be crucial for agency survival. Agencies need to make better estimates of their true overhead costs so that they do not, on average, lose money as a result of government funding. The 'cause of voluntarism' would also be better served if Boards of Governors would be more actively involved in communication with government and in the formulation of policy relating to the execution of government contracts.

Whereas other authors (for example, *Berg and Wright*) have pointed to the possible impact of government funding on agency goals, this study draws attention to problems of *managing governmental funds*. The possibility that voluntary agencies are undervaluing their true overhead costs when receiving government funds, has only recently received attention in Britain (see *Judge*).

J. Hasler, 'Quandaries of Participation', *MDU Bulletin*, 3/4, July 1984, pp. 14–15.

Using the example of the Children's Society 'Family Centres', this article describes some of the organisational problems that can arise when local projects involve their users as partners rather than as clients. The idea of participation is

48

unfamiliar to the national agency's world of formal procedures in which use and control of services are separated.

The author argues that his agency needs 'a new picture' which starts from an acceptance of 'the *interrelation* of consumption and control' and portrays the agency 'as a series of partnerships, each of which could be organised as a negotiating arena'.

S. Hatch, *Voluntary Work: A Report of a Survey*, Volunteer Centre, 1978.

This paper reports on a survey conducted for the *Wolfenden Committee* and later discussed in a book by the author *(Hatch, 1980 (1))*.

S. Hatch, *Outside the State – Voluntary Organisations in Three English Towns*, Croom Helm, 1980 (1).

This book reports a comparative and longitudinal study of voluntary organisations in three English towns, part of which was carried out for the *Wolfenden Committee*. The study findings are related throughout the book to wider issues about growth and change in the voluntary sector, the role of the voluntary sector, and the relationship between voluntary organisations and local authorities.

'Voluntary organisations' are defined in negative terms as groups not established by statutes or under statutory authority and which are not commercial or profit-making. Hatch reviews some of the many ways in which voluntary organisations may be classified and goes on to propose his own classification based on the resources used by voluntary organisations in carrying out their work. He distinguishes mutual aid associations, volunteer organisations, special agencies (using paid staff and grants), and funded charities.

Hatch says that since the 1940s there has been no growth or a decline in voluntary sector activity in the fields of education, family planning, adoption and services for the deaf and blind. Growth has occurred among organisations dealing with people with specific handicaps, playgroups, advice and counselling services, neighbourhood organisations, and housing, ethnic and environmental organisations. The most common trigger to voluntary development is deliberate action by the personnel of statutory or existing voluntary agencies, but new agencies also develop from spontaneous individual or group action, church sponsorship or outgrowth from an existing voluntary organisation.

Although the kernel of this book is provided by the study findings, and the discussion about the role of the voluntary sector in welfare provision (see also *Hadley and Hatch, 1981*), its main relevance for the student of organisational issues lies in the *search for typologies* of voluntary organisations and for a better understanding of the nature of growth.

S. Hatch (ed), *Mutual Aid and Social and Health Care*, Bedford Square Press/NCVO, 1980 (2).

This booklet is a collection of papers which arose from the 1978 conference of ARVAC (Association for Research into Voluntary and Community Action).

In his introductory essay Hatch distinguishes between self-help, in which the emphasis is on self-interested action, and mutual aid, in which the emphasis is on co-operative endeavour. Mutual aid may occur within families, geographical areas or organisations. In the case of organisations, it is not always possible to distinguish between a member, who is a beneficiary of mutual aid, and a client who is a beneficiary of the service.

Drawing on his own research (*Hatch, 1980 (1)*) the author suggests that the number of mutual aid and self-help groups is increasing, although their coverage of need is patchy. Three main categories of mutual aid and self-help groups are playgroups and mothers and toddlers groups; clubs for the elderly; and a residual category dealing with medical problems, handicap and single parents. Groups may also be categorised according to the strategy they use; whether they aim to change their own participants or society generally, or whether they wish to change attitudes or make material provision. Playgroups, for example, aim to change their own participants through material provision. The Campaign for Homosexual Equality, on the other hand, wants to change society's attitudes.

S. Hatch, 'The Voluntary Sector: A Larger Role', in E. M. Goldberg and S. Hatch (eds), *A New Look at the Personal Social Services*, Policy Studies Institute (PSI), 1981.

This paper discusses the scope for growth in the voluntary sector. It suggests that a more 'plural pattern' of social provision is possible but that more resources are essential since the voluntary sector cannot compensate for public expenditure cuts.

S. Hatch (ed), *Volunteers: Patterns, Meanings and Motives*, Volunteer Centre, 1982.

This symposium brings together reports of several research projects concerned broadly with volunteering and voluntarism.

S. Hatch: see also p. 42 (two entries).

S. Hatch and I. Mocroft, 'Factors Affecting the Location of Voluntary Organisation Branches', *Policy and Politics*, 6, 1977, pp. 163–172.

This article describes a part of the research which was done for the *Wolfenden Committee*. The study reported here examined the location of branches of 22 national voluntary organisations in all towns in England and Wales which had a population of over 50,000 in 1971. The towns were classified according to 26 indicators of social and economic conditions.

Voluntary organisation branches were more likely to be found in some towns than others. This was partly due to chance but the largest explanatory factor for location was the presence in a town of a large proportion of people in higher social classes. Thus, often the towns in which needs were greatest were least well served by national voluntary organisations. The authors conclude that 'social policies relying on voluntary organisations as instruments of policy will be uneven in their impact in the absence of successful attempts to stimulate the voluntary sector in areas poorly endowed with organisations'.

For voluntary agencies, the matching of social need to available manpower and other resources can be highly problematic. (See, for example, *Abrams et al, 1981*.) The limiting factors identified by the authors will be of considerable interest to those concerned with establishing branches of larger voluntary agencies.

S. Hatch and I. Mocroft, 'The Relative Costs of Services Provided by Voluntary and Statutory Organisations', *Public Administration*, 57, Winter 1979, pp. 397–405.

This article reports a study which further developed work originally done for the *Wolfenden Committee* on the comparative costs of statutory and voluntary sector provision of welfare services. It draws on data about children's homes, the building and maintenance of rented accommodation, hostels for single people, and women's refuges.

The authors argue that 'even when paid staff are being used the voluntary organisation can exhibit considerable cost advantages. The advantages are attributable to various factors. The organisation may have lower overheads and it may meet need in a way that is intrinsically less expensive than the work done by comparable statutory organisations. But the main factor seems to be the greater commitment that a voluntary organisation can in some circumstances elicit from its staff, and their consequent willingness to work harder and/or for less money than the equivalent staff in a statutory organisation.'

Commenting on their findings, the authors point out that the cost advantages of voluntary agencies may be eroded as the need for the service becomes more accepted, procedures become 'routinised' and 'professionalised' and funders seek more formally-structured systems of accountability. Staff become less committed and less willing to work for low wages.

The authors conclude that administrators should be more tolerant of 'less bureaucratised' forms of provision, not only because they are likely to be cheaper but also because 'non-hierarchical moral communities' may be a better instrument for pursuing some aspects of human development.

This article illustrates clearly the close inter-relationship between the organisation and management of voluntary agencies and broader issues of social policy. (See also *Billis, 1984 (1)*). It suggests that consideration of a larger role for voluntary agencies in welfare service provision cannot be separated from an understanding of their internal administration. And questions about relative costs of the statutory and voluntary sectors are shown to be more complex than may have at first appeared.

S. Hatch and I. Mocroft, 'The Politics of Partnership', *Voluntary Action*, Autumn 1982, pp. 28–29.

This article provides a summary of the authors' book (*Hatch and Mocroft, 1983*).

S. Hatch and I. Mocroft, *Components of Welfare: Voluntary Organisations, Social Services and Politics in Two Local Authorities*, Bedford Square Press/NCVO, 1983.

This book reports a research study commissioned by the Personal Social Services Council and carried out during one year 1978–79. The general area of interest was the relationship between voluntary organisations and local authorities, with the main focus on Social Services departments' policy and practice towards other sectors. The departments studied were in Islington and Suffolk.

The characteristics of the voluntary sector in the two areas differed. In Suffolk, voluntary organisations tended to have firmly defined structures and were able to mobilise volunteers to provide services. Voluntary sector action was often a substitute for statutory services. In Islington, on the other hand, many voluntary organisations were recently developed with young paid staff funded by local authority grants. Generally voluntary sector action complemented local authority services, acted as an alternative focus for social services and/or initiated new services for the area.

Four routine procedures used by Social Services departments to maintain the accountability to them of voluntary agencies were identified: collecting information for grant-making; retaining control over referral of clients; council inspection; and the application of professional standards. But the local authorities studied avoided tight control or 'routinised administrative procedures'. Instead they tended to rely on obtaining a general impression of an organisation's affairs through informal contacts and networks.

P. Henderson and P. Taylor, *Voluntarism: A Practitioner View*, Association of Community Workers, 1982.

This booklet addresses the dilemma of how an extension of voluntary effort and community action might be reconciled with the maintenance of the quality of the welfare state. It expresses concern that when the state draws on informal networks, as advocated by the *Barclay Working Party*, it colonises rather than supports them.

52

S. Henry: see p. 83.

R. Herzlinger: see p. 14.

N. Hinton, 'An Outlet for Change, Creative Innovation and Improvement', *Voluntary Action*, Autumn, 1980, p. 4.

This article argues that voluntary organisations need continued financial support. Good practice depends on an efficient, well-ordered infrastructure that is able to recruit, prepare, deploy, support and replace volunteers.

N. Hinton and M. Hyde, 'The Voluntary Sector in a Remodelled Welfare State', in C. Jones and J. Stevenson (eds), *Yearbook of Social Policy in Britain, 1980–81*, Routledge and Kegan Paul, 1982.

This article focuses not on 'the formal facts of structure and funding' in the voluntary sector, but on social policy issues which relate to the sector, such as responsiveness to needs, accountability and participation. The authors argue for a 'decentralised, pluralist approach' to meeting human needs.

HMSO, *50 Million Volunteers: Report on the Role of Voluntary Organisations and Youth in the Environment*, HMSO, 1972.

This book reports a study of public opinion undertaken in connection with the United Nations Conference on the Human Environment, Stockholm, 1972. Although it is mainly concerned with youth and environment, it includes some comments and recommendations about volunteers and voluntary movements generally. It suggests that voluntary movements could improve their efficiency through mergers and sharing of facilities, through greater use of willing professional or skilled helpers, and by paying greater attention to leadership and job training.

D. Hobman, 'Cause Rather Than Concept', *Health and Social Services Journal*, 11 July, 1980, pp. 913–915.

This article gives a personal viewpoint on the voluntary sector role. Arguing that the sector is 'a replacement for vanishing support networks in the contemporary idiom', the author suggests that its main influence on society 'is felt by what it does, rather than what it says'.

Volunteers' commitment to specific organisations arises from emotional causes rather than concepts and so rivalry rather than co-operation between voluntary organisations operating in similar fields is inevitable. Yet some co-operation, rationalisation and common fund-raising appeals are nevertheless essential.

A. Holme and J. Maizels, *Social Workers and Volunteers*, British Association of Social Workers and Allen and Unwin, 1978.

This book reports the results of a national survey of social workers which aimed to discover the ways in which they used volunteers and how they perceived the role of volunteers. The discussion is restricted to the involvement of volunteers in statutory services.

Home Office Voluntary Services Unit, *The Government and the Voluntary Sector: An Analysis of the Response to the Consultative Document*, Home Office, 1981.

This booklet presents, in summary form, the answers given to a series of questions in a consultative document on the *Wolfenden Committee Report*. Chapter 6 reviews aspects of monitoring voluntary agencies' activities and Chapter 7, entitled 'Oversight', deals with the relationship between voluntary agencies and outside funders.

S. Humble, *Voluntary Action in the 1980s: A Summary of the Findings of a National Survey*, Volunteer Centre, 1982.

This booklet is the final report of a national survey of volunteering in Britain, funded by the SSRC. (The pilot survey was reported by B. Mostyn in *Hatch (ed), 1982*.) Topics covered include public perceptions of voluntary work, numbers involved, time spent on volunteering, what volunteers do, and their reasons for involvement.

R. Humphrey: see p. 12.

M. Hyde: see p. 53.

S. Hyman, *The Management of Associations*, CBD Research Ltd., 1979.

This book, according to its author, 'is about managing organisations such as clubs, community centres, churches, housing associations, trade associations and professional institutions'. Its aim is to analyse the 'challenges of management' in associations as seen by two 'key forces'; namely, committee members and officers and the paid officials.

The author emphasises throughout the need for rigorous efforts to define the goals of the organisation and to identify the resources it needs if the goals are to be achieved. Several other issues which arise in voluntary associations are discussed and the author presents his own views and prescriptions. In relation to meeting members' needs, for example, he argues that participation by members and democratic structures are less important than ensuring that the committee and officials are aware of, and responsive to, members' needs.

As regards the choice between informality and growth which faces successful associations, Hyman says that 'If informality is preferred, the association must stay small, and recruitment above the chosen maximum must be refused', but that such such a decision will be impossible for most organisations which want to influence events.

Other organisational and management problems identified and addressed by the author include the disciplining of volunteers; the reluctance to take a business-like approach to financial affairs; the high value attached to muddled working procedures; and the need for collaboration between associations to provide career opportunities for paid officials.

This book is a significant contribution to the modest body of U.K. literature, addressed primarily to voluntary sector *managers*. (See also works by *Feek* and *Hackney Community Action*.) The more detailed prescriptive statements may need to be approached with circumspection and tested against the realities of individual agencies' situations.

Information Service for Voluntary Organisations
A monthly news-sheet published by NCVO and discontinued in December 1983.

A. James, 'An Institutional Experiment in the Amelioration of Race Relations – The Dilemma of a Voluntary Organisation', in R. Olsen (ed), *Management in the Social Services – The Team Leader's Task*, Occasional Papers No. 1, University College of North Wales, Bangor, 1975, pp. 42–56.

This paper provides a case study of a voluntary agency established in 1954 by a local Council of Social Service to give 'welfare' to immigrants. It describes how the agency, originally established to provide individual casework and counselling, gradually moved to a community focus in its work, in response to demands from immigrants for more involvement and to their need for different kinds of services (e.g. housing and employment advice and facilities for children and young people).

B. Jerman, *The Lively Minded Women*, Heinemann, 1982.

This book is an account of the development of the National Housewives Register (NHR) since 1960 when the first mutual support group for housebound women was started following a letter to the *Guardian* newspaper. By 1980, NHR had 21,000 members in 1,000 neighbourhood groups.

55

The account shows clearly the critical stages in NHR's growth and the problems and dilemmas accompanying each stage. After the first few years of rapid growth, there were, for example, debates about who should be eligible for membership; whether NHR should move from self-help to be a pressure group; whether it had a distinctive purpose; and whether some regional levels of organisation were needed. Again, up to 1976, there was no form of membership voting for the National Group, and National Organisers appointed their own successors. In that year a constitution was formally adopted largely to protect officers and their families from financial liability, but which also clarified and formalised some of NHR's structure and decision-making processes.

At the time when the book was written, on its 20th anniversary in 1980, NHR had no salaried director nor any regional level of administration. Its members remained committed to retaining informality and spontaneity within a non-hierarchical 'unorganised organisation'.

The main interest of this book lies in the description and analysis of the dilemmas facing a large organisation which takes an explicit decision not to move from the informal world towards service-delivery and bureaucratic organisation. The study of Riverside (*Billis, 1984 (2)*) illustrates similar tensions in a growing self-help group.

N. Johnson, 'What Sort of Service?', *Social Service Quarterly*, 51, 3, Jan.-March 1978, pp. 85–88 (1).

Drawing on the work of a number of writers (including *Gordon and Babchuk*), this article examines possible typologies of voluntary social services. Johnson says that no single typology is likely to be appropriate for all purposes and that it might be possible to combine a number of typologies in developing a description of any particular organisation.

The author suggests that voluntary social service agencies may be classified according to:

- objectives or primary purpose
- accessibility of membership
- status-defining capacity
- whether their functions are instrumental or expressive
- the levels (national or local) at which they operate
- the relationship between the levels (federal or corporate).

This article is a useful review of possible bases for classifying voluntary social services. (See *Wolfenden Committee Report* and *Hatch, 1980 (1)* for a discussion of a method of classifying the voluntary sector as a whole.) Johnson's use of the term 'typology' may cause some difficulties since no distinction is made between a typology such as that proposed by *Gordon and Babchuk*, which is based on a number of variables, and single classificatory criteria or factors which are also referred to by Johnson as 'typologies'.

N. Johnson, 'The Finance of Voluntary Organisations for the Physically Disabled', *Social and Economic Administration*, 12, 3, Winter 1978, pp. 169–81 (2).

This article provides an analysis of the annual accounts, finances and fundraising methods of 15 voluntary organisations.

N. Johnson, *Voluntary Social Services*, Blackwell and Robinson, 1981.

This book reviews various aspects of the provision of personal social services by non-statutory voluntary agencies. Government policies for encouraging voluntary organisations to provide more such services give a context for much of the discussion.

An early chapter suggests that voluntary agencies may be defined in terms of their methods of formation (people come together voluntarily); their method of government (self-governing with no legal obligations to provide services); their method of finance (some from voluntary sources); and their motives (non-profit-making). Some typologies of voluntary social services agencies are proposed (see also *Johnson, 1978 (1)*). But the author points out that, in practice, the line between statutory and voluntary provision is blurred by the fact that professional staff have similar backgrounds in both types of agency; by the assistance given to voluntary agencies by statutory ones; and by the close working relationships that have arisen between the two sectors, particularly since the Seebohm Report was implemented.

The chapter on 'Pioneering' discusses the case for a continuing pioneering role for voluntary social services and points out that statutory bodies can also be pioneering (CDPs were an example), and that inertia may set in in voluntary bodies, just as in statutory ones.

Many social policy issues are raised by the author. He wonders about the effects of government funding and partnerships with statutory agencies on the traditional independence of voluntary organisations. In a concluding chapter, he points out that arguments for a wider role for voluntary organisations must be set within the context of their uneven distribution, weak accountability, questionable internal democracy and their middle-class bias.

Arguments in favour of an expanded voluntary sector role in welfare service provision have mostly been debated in rather negative terms (the statutory sector is inadequate), and/or in terms of held values (the voluntary sector promotes community and participation or is a bulwark against encroaching state bureaucracy). This book enters the debate from a different angle, that of the *organisational features* of voluntary agencies themselves.

D. Jones: see p. 94.

P. Jones: see p. 29.

Journal of Voluntary Action Research.
This is the journal of the United States Association of Voluntary Action Scholars, usually published quarterly. It is obtainable from Box G-55, Boston College, Chestnut Hill, Mass. 02167, U.S.A.

K. Judge, 'The Public Purchase of Social Care: British Confirmation of the American Experience', *Policy and Politics*, **10, 4, October 1982, pp. 397–416.**

Purchase of Service Contracting (POSC) has been increasingly used by the United States government since the 1970s. The purpose of this article is to relate the United States experience to England. It reviews the arguments for and against POSC, clarifies what forms POSC can take and makes a preliminary assessment of how POSC is working in England at present. It compares this picture with U.S. literature and discusses some of the possible implications of an expansion of POSC in England.

Four types of POSC are distinguished:

- Vendor reimbursement for client-specific services, such as places in residential homes
- Proportional reimbursement of costs to delegate agencies
- Major grants for quasi-contracting by a local authority
- Minor grants in support of general community development.

POSC can be managed or monitored in two ways. Fiscal monitoring (contract compliance and financial auditing) is commonly used by social services departments. It is highly visible and thought to be effective. The second possibility, programme monitoring, has only been developed in a very rudimentary way, although it would probably be appropriate to most forms of POSC except the purchase of residential care where there is a 'professional social work interest' in individual clients.

The author found little evidence that POSC in England poses any threat to the autonomy of voluntary organisations, thus apparently confirming U.S. experience. In fact, Judge suggests that, by subsidising public purchases, voluntary organisations involved in POSC actually increase their own relative power.

J. A. Kahle, 'Structuring and Administering a Modern Voluntary Agency', *Social Work*, **14, 4, October 1969, pp. 21–28.**

The thesis of this article is that voluntary social work agencies in the United States are 'over-institutionalised' and have an 'archaic' structure. Part of the problem is seen to be that responsibility for administration is 'in the hands of amateur managers recruited from the ranks of social work practitioners'.

Kahle contrasts bureaucratic, pyramidal structures borrowed from business and industry, with alternative, 'collegial', structures, a system which he thinks is unworkable in practice. All social workers are not equally capable of assuming full responsibility for their own practice; they need leadership. 'In addition, no organisation or agency with a publicly sanctioned purpose and function can operate without direction, control and responsibility.'

Kahle argues that a workable structure for voluntary social work agencies would be a pyramidal-collegial one, comprising a 'broad rectangle topped by a flattened pyramid'. This would reduce the administrative structure and increase the proportion of direct service staff. Basic managerial control as in a bureaucratic system would be maintained, but there would also be the two-way communication of the collegial system.

G. N. Karn, 'The Business of Boards is Serious Business', *Voluntary Action Leadership*, Winter 1983, pp. 14–19.

This article, written by the director of a voluntary agency, argues that members of boards (governing bodies) faced with the dilemmas caused by cutbacks in resources should give their full attention to their own primary responsibilities. These include:

- Administration of the agency
- Programme planning and budgeting
- Evaluation of organisational effectiveness and mission achievement
- Retention and performance evaluation of top management
- Financial stewardship
- 'Constituting the Community Connection'.

The writer emphasises the importance of conscientiousness among board members in carrying out these functions since it is 'a natural law of organizational dynamics' that when a board of directors abdicates its responsibilities, staff will move in to fill the void in the balance of power.

A. H. Katz, 'Self-Help Organisations and Volunteer Participation in Social Welfare', *Social Work*, 15, 1, January 1970, pp. 51–61.

The study reported in this paper was an analysis of self-help groups in the health and welfare fields using the standpoint of small-group, organisational and sociological theories.

The author suggests that self-help groups are a new kind of social agency that must be considered as a part of the voluntary sector. They are distinguished from the more conventional philanthropic social agencies by the fact that they are self-organised and that their origins lie in mutual aid. In type they may be 'assimilative', 'separative' or 'mixed'.

Drawing on other literature, Katz identifies eight distinctive structural features of self-help organisations. They are similar to small groups in that they offer individual satisfactions; they are problem-centred; members tend to be peers and to hold common goals; the aim is to help others and action is group action; the role of the professional is not clear-cut; and power and leadership is on a horizontal basis among peers. Functional attributes flow from these structural features. Communication is horizontal rather than vertical, personal involvement and responsibility is required and the group is action orientated.

Using his own analysis over time of some self-help groups, Katz suggests that such groups move from informal organisation to the stage of emergence of leaders. Gradually formal rules and roles are developed and eventually there is professionalisation, with a shift in administrative and service functions from volunteers to staff. But he argues that, in spite of professionalisation, groups which begin as self-help groups retain a distinctiveness: 'volunteer functions in these groups remain broader, more intensive, and more varied than in the more conventional private social agency'.

This article is a part of the U.S. literature which has attempted to discover underlying patterns in the growth of organisations. It follows in the tradition of *Chapin and Tsouderos* and may be contrasted with more recent U.K. literature which takes a problem-orientated approach and also questions the inevitability of professionalisation and formalisation. (See, for example, *Billis*, *1984 (2)* and *Mellett*.)

J. P. Keathley: see p. 35.

J. N. Kerri, 'Studying Voluntary Associations as Adaptive Mechanisms: A Review of Anthropological Perspectives', *Current Anthropology*, 17, 1, March 1976, pp. 23–34.

This article argues from an anthropological viewpoint, that voluntary associations are a type of common interest group and that they are particularly attractive now because they are 'more pliable than kinship or territorial units in situations of social, cultural or technological change'.

C. W. King, 'Career Patterns of Social Movements' in W. A. Glaser and D. L. Sills (eds), *The Government of Associations*, Bedminster Press, Totowa, New Jersey, 1966. (ILL)

This paper points out that agencies which try to change society may be organised expressions of broader social movements. The author goes on to describe how social movements move from their original 'incipient phase' to an 'organizational phase' in which division of labour, specialisation, hierarchies and specific behavioural norms emerge. Finally, there is a 'stable phase' in which organisation, ideology and tactics become clearcut and orderly. There is a transition from the original charismatic staff to legitimated authority.

An editorial comment following this paper points out the relevance of King's descriptions for the study of the voluntary sector. Voluntary associations may develop during organisational or stable phases of social movements. Those which arise during the organisational phase experience rapid expansion of activities, high turnover of members and donors, and conflicts between charismatic leaders and new professional staff. There are also conflicting pulls between desires for stabilisation and change of goals. Voluntary associations which arise in the later, stable, phase, however, may suffer from complacency. The problem of leaders then, is 'to prevent both employees and volunteers from becoming pre-occupied with the organisation's affairs to the neglect of its goals'.

S. Kingsley, 'Voluntary Action: Innovation and Experiment as Criteria for Funding', *Home Office Research Bulletin*, 11, 1981, pp. 7–10.

This article, based on the experiences of the Home Office Research Unit, considers 'the extent to which voluntary organisations produce innovative and experimental programmes'. It argues that, apart from identifying new client groups and needs, their innovative role is limited (see also *Kramer, 1979 (1)*). Nevertheless, they tend to receive funding for experimental periods only on the assumption that this *is* their prime role. 'This leads to numerous problems in the development of programmes and places unnecessary pressures' on them.

R. M. Kramer, 'Ideology, Status and Power in Board-Executive Relationships', *Social Work*, 10, October 1965, pp. 107–114.

The key question addressed by this article is 'How does the voluntary agency manage to function in the face of apparent welfare value conflicts and status and power disparities in its policy-making "team"?'

Drawing on studies and writings by himself and others, Kramer identifies a series of factors which serve to prevent or minimise ideological conflict in voluntary agencies. These factors include the substantive, non-ideological character of most necessary decision-making, and the use of mechanisms within agencies to reduce possible disruptive effects. Staff, for example, may introduce only safe issues for board consideration, and board members may act and vote in accordance with community interests rather than their own socio-economic class interests.

Kramer argues that a balance of power between governing bodies and paid directors ('Boards' and 'Executive Directors') is maintained by the 'exchange' nature of their relationship. There is a mutual dependency, since the Executive Director 'requires the sanction and support of the Board members and the latter, in turn, gain prestige and validation of their position as community leaders'. Equilibrium is also maintained by the 'process of selective recruitment and self-perpetuation of members for whom the agency had relatively low salience and who will not be inclined to disrupt the ongoing pattern of board-executive relationships'.

The main interest of this article lies in its exploration of the inter-relationship between the way in which voluntary agencies function and the motivations of members of their governing bodies.

R. M. Kramer, 'Voluntary Agencies and the Use of Public Funds: Some Policy Issues', *Social Service Review*, 40, March 1966, pp. 15–26.

This paper discusses the circumstances under which it may be considered appropriate for voluntary agencies to receive different types of public funds (e.g. through purchase of service, subsidies, grants, contracts or fees).

It points out that there are organisational implications for voluntary agencies of receiving governmental funding. Some form of governmental control is inevitably involved and there is necessarily a strain between the governmental agency's need to assure public accountability and the voluntary agency's requirement for autonomy. The dilemma is that 'limited organisational autonomy is functional from the community's perspective, but dysfunctional from the agency's point of view'.

R. M. Kramer, 'Alternative Futures for Voluntary Agencies in Social Welfare', *Journal of Voluntary Action Research*, 6, 1–2, 1977, pp. 18–22.

In this article Kramer distinguishes four different types of non-governmental human service agency 'based on the degree of reliance on governmental funding and consumer involvement in policy-making': private agencies, quangos, alternative agencies and vendors.

Each type of agency is seen as differing with regard to fiscal support, area of interest and organisational structure. The agencies in the different groups therefore have different futures, although Kramer argues that all of them will come under pressure to provide 'higher levels of managerial efficiency, accountability and effectiveness'.

R. M. Kramer, 'The Voluntary Agency in the Welfare State: an analysis of the Vanguard Role', *Journal of Social Policy*, 8, 4, 1979, pp. 473–488 (1).

Pioneering is assumed to be a unique function of voluntary agencies. This article draws on a study of 20 English agencies serving the physically and mentally handicapped to examine the extent of the pioneering or 'vanguard' role in voluntary agencies.

The author found that much of what is regarded as innovative in voluntary agencies consists, in fact, of small-scale, non-controversial, incremental improvements or is an extension to existing programmes. The norm is programme change or modification rather than an original, first-of-a-kind mode of intervention or service delivery. But because innovation is highly valued in society, especially by funders, an emphasis tends to be placed on pioneering at the expense of other important aspects of voluntary agency activity such as access and choice for clients or effectiveness in performance.

Where programmes are initiated by voluntary agencies, they may then be continued by the original sponsor, adopted by other organisations, transferred to a statutory body, or cease altogether. The author shows that there are a series of external and internal organisational constraints on statutory adoption of new programmes. Internally, an agency may be opposed to state activity or reluctant to give up a good fund-raiser. Statutory bodies, on the other hand, may be reluctant to adopt services for minorities or controversial causes. They may also experience difficulties arising from their incongruent boundaries with voluntary agencies.

The author suggests that it is the small voluntary organisations in an early stage of development which are most likely to discover under-served or specialist needs. Governmental and more established voluntary agencies might then introduce new modes of intervention.

This article indicates the subtlety of the inter-relationship between funders' requirements and policy development in voluntary agencies. It also provides an empirical underpinning to the debate about the innovative role of the voluntary sector (see also *Kingsley*).

R. M. Kramer, 'Public Fiscal Policy and Voluntary Agencies in Welfare States', *Social Service Review*, 53, March 1979, pp. 1–14 (2).

The focus of this article is on those voluntary agencies which, at least in the United States, deliver a growing proportion of governmentally-financed personal social services, through contract purchase arrangements. They are part of a 'mixed economy' of welfare in a 'contract state'. The question arises as to how accountable they can be to their funders while, at the same time, retaining their independence.

Using material derived from his cross-national study of voluntary agencies (see *Kramer, 1981*) the author shows how the relationship pattern between the government and voluntary sectors varies greatly between countries, as does the percentage of their total income which voluntary agencies derive from governmental sources.

Little evidence was found that government funds are inherently 'corrupting, coopting or constraining' for voluntary agencies. Four possible reasons are that public funds are frequently provided in the form of payment for services; voluntary agencies often have a number of different income sources; voluntary agencies provide a countervailing power of service monopoly and political influence; and governments accept low accountability because they are dependent on voluntary agencies.

It is concluded that the organisational outcomes of government financing of voluntary agency services depend on the conditions under which the funds are made available, their amount, their duration, the proportion they form of the total agency budget, the number and diversity of fund sources, and the type of accountability required.

Kramer argues that 'bureaucratic symbiosis' or 'mutual cooptation', in which both parties recognise their interdependence, may be good for both government and voluntary sectors. But it is not necessarily of benefits to clients who might prefer voluntary agencies to be more accountable to them. Kramer suggests that it might, therefore, be preferable for voluntary agencies to perform less long-term service provision and to concentrate more on 'articulation of interests'.

This article contributes to the debate about the effects of government funding on the internal working of voluntary agencies (see also comment on *Rosenbaum*).

R. M. Kramer, *Voluntary Agencies in the Welfare State*, University of California Press, 1981.

The author of this book studied 80 voluntary agencies for the physically and mentally handicapped in England, the United States, the Netherlands and Israel. His concern was with those voluntary agencies that are 'essentially bureaucratic' and which employ professional or volunteer staff to provide a welfare service. He examined the welfare context within which the agencies worked in each country and he also looked at the agencies' organisational structures with regard, for example, to size, formalisation, professionalisation, system of government, policy-making, funding and control.

Kramer identifies four roles with which voluntary organisations are widely associated: namely, pioneer, advocate or improver, service-provider and promoter of participation, or voluntarism. He then examines the factors which influence how these roles are executed by voluntary agencies in each of the four countries.

The study's findings raise some doubts about the extent to which voluntary agencies are able to innovate or offer alternatives to state provision. They also confirm that voluntary agencies have a tendency to minority rule and to staff domination in decision-making. In addition, they allay some of the fears about the constraining effect of public funding on voluntary agencies.

On the basis of his findings, Kramer offers some suggestions as to where the distinctive features of the voluntary sector really do and should lie. He argues that specialisation is a more salient attribute of voluntary agencies than pioneering or innovation, and that service provision is the least distinctive function. Moreover, he thinks that the provision of services, especially on behalf of statutory authorities, may deflect an agency from the more distinctive function of advocacy or pressure-group activity.

Finally, Kramer identifies four characteristic 'vulnerabilities' of voluntary agencies; namely institutionalisation, goal deflection, minority rule and ineffectuality.

This book represents the final report of a large study, some interim results of which were published earlier in articles on particular topics (for example in *Kramer, 1979 (1)* and *Kramer, 1979 (2)*). The report is unusual and especially valuable, not only because its arguments are based on empirical material, but also because it focuses explicitly on describing *organisational aspects* of the voluntary sector; for example, the organisational implications of growth and relations between staff and their governing bodies.

64

The framework it provides for analysing the roles and distinctive features of voluntary agencies has already been noted and used as a basis for analysis by others (see, for example, *Scott, 1982*). It also paves the way for further research and theory development.

S. Kurowska, 'Meeting the Challenge', *Voluntary Action*, Spring, 1983, pp. 24–25.

This article describes area resource centres which provide equipment and technical expertise for community groups. The relationships between area resource centres and Councils of Voluntary Service is considered. The article concludes with the suggestion that community groups and voluntary agencies need access not only to hardware but also to 'professional and technical services such as community, accountancy, legal, management, or architectural services'.

J. A. LaCour, 'Organizational Structure: Implications for Volunteer Program Outcome', *Journal of Voluntary Action Research*, 6, 1–2, 1977, pp. 41–47.

The main focus of this article is on motivating and administering volunteers in projects or programs, but the author also makes some suggestions about the organisational structures which facilitate successful volunteer programs.

J. E. Lane, *The Motivations of Full-Time Workers in Voluntary Agencies*, M.Sc. Thesis, Cranfield Institute of Technology, 1981.

This thesis reports a research study of what motivates people to become employees of voluntary agencies, rather than business, commerce or the public services. A quota sample of 10 voluntary agencies was taken and workers who were about to join the agencies were invited to participate in the research. Those who accepted (80 per cent = 32 people) were interviewed twice; before beginning their job and three months after beginning it. The data obtained was used to answer three questions:

- What reasons lead people to work in voluntary agencies?
- What sources of satisfaction and dissatisfaction are found there?
- What factors lead them to remain in or leave voluntary agencies?

The study findings suggested that 'if altruism is understood to mean the self-forgetting service of others, there is little sign of it being either sought or found in voluntary agencies'. The main and distinctive motivation of staff interviewed was their need for 'self-actualisation' – a need which they seemed prepared to put before their needs for good pay, status or consumer durables. The researcher found that 'people join voluntary agencies mainly for what they get out of it, to work with people of like mind, to develop personal skills and abilities, to gain more personal freedom'.

The author concludes with some practical suggestions about how staff needs for self-actualisation may be met within the organisational structure of a voluntary agency, for example, by participative management systems.

Although the motivations of volunteer workers have been studied and debated in recent years (see for example, *Leat, 1978* and *Hatch* (ed), *1982*), the motivations of *employed staff* in the voluntary sector have received little attention.

J. Lansley, *Voluntary Organisations Facing Change*, Calouste Gulbenkian Foundation and Joseph Rowntree Memorial Trust, 1976.

This booklet is the final report of a research project designed to assist Community Councils (later Councils for Voluntary Service) to develop in ways appropriate to the changed pattern of local government in the new Metropolitan Counties of Greater Manchester and Merseyside.

The researcher started with the Community Councils Development Group's ideal model of the functions, clientele and formal structure of a new Council for Voluntary Service (CVS), but encountered many problems in attempting to put the model into practice. One problem was to create organisational structures that would be effective at both district and local level. Another was the conflict between the desire to set up a number of CVSs quickly and the wish to help existing organisations to develop and adapt to local government change. A third problem was how to employ full-time professional staff without losing the interest and commitment of lay members of the governing executive committees. Lansley is thus led to suggest that the project demonstrates the importance of distinguishing between the formal constitution of an agency and its actual structures.

Lansley also demonstrates the importance of the relationship between an organisation's goals and ideology on the one hand, and its structure on the other. The theoretical model envisaged both promotional and co-ordinative functions for the new CVS. However, the project showed that these two functions required different organisational structures and were, therefore, mutually exclusive. The co-ordinative approach suggested a unitary organisation controlled by representatives of the member organisations. The self-help, promotional approach, on the other hand, was consistent with a pluralist ideology of voluntary groups using the CVS as a consultant and an open forum for their competing and different interests and ideas for action.

Although the reorganisation of local government and the accompanying organisational upheavals are no longer new, this report of an action-research project remains of interest for the insights it gives into the problems of achieving *organisational change* in the voluntary sector. It also illustrates clearly the constraints on goal-implementation which can be set by organisational structure.

A more recent study by *Leat et al* of intermediary bodies also describes the practical difficulties of combining co-ordinating and promotional aims within one agency.

J. Lansley, *Structure and Dynamics of Voluntary Organisations*. Paper presented to the SSRC Workshop, 'Research on the Voluntary Sector', SSRC, 1979. (Available on loan from SSRC/ESRC Library.)

This short paper suggests some questions to which organisational research in voluntary agencies might address itself.

It begins by pointing out that studies of voluntary organisations in Britain have tended to concentrate on issues of participation and social policy. Structural aspects of voluntary agencies – the 'organisational context' – have been largely ignored. Moreover the uncertain boundaries of the voluntary sector make it difficult to apply many of the findings of organisational studies of other areas except in a rather tentative way.

Organisational research in voluntary agencies might be addressed to questions about the formation of agencies and factors in their survival. As regards the structure and dynamics of voluntary agencies, questions are raised about their constitutions; the degree and effect of bureaucratisation and professionalisation within them; federations and branches; and relationships with other organisations. Lansley suggests that there should be studies of individual agencies or broader comparative studies 'perhaps particularly testing out how far some of the findings of other organisational studies may be relevant in the fields of organisational change and inter-organisational relationships'.

Law Reform Committee, *The Powers and Duties of Trustees*, Twenty-Third Report, Cmnd. 8733, HMSO, 1982.

This report includes a discussion of the distinction between 'trustees' and 'charity trustees' and considers the powers and duties of charity trustees.

D. Leat, *Research Into Community Involvement*, Volunteer Centre, 1977.

This directory of research completed or in progress in 1977, precedes the one compiled by *Selwyn*.

D. Leat, *Towards a Definition of Volunteer Involvement*, Volunteer Centre, 1978.

In this booklet Leat examines three possible ways of understanding voluntary work and concludes that it may be more appropriate to think of volunteering as 'quasi-friendship', as this recognises the goal of mutual caring in society.

D. Leat and G. Darvill, *Voluntary Visiting: A Review and Discussion of Methods of Organisation of Voluntary Visiting of the Elderly*, Volunteer Centre, 1977.

This booklet reviews the findings of research projects concerned with provision of voluntary visiting services for the elderly, with a view to clarifying 'how and under what circumstances volunteers may help'.

It suggests that visiting schemes may be categorised according to the kind of help given; the range of help; the type of volunteer; degree of formalisation of activity; the location of the scheme's focal point for contacts; and the degree of interdependence with the statutory services.

A discussion of the research findings on co-ordination and the role of co-ordinators emphasises the need for organisation and structure even for groups and schemes committed to informality, flexibility, spontaneity, and voluntarism.

D. Leat, G. Smolka and J. Unell, *Voluntary and Statutory Collaboration, Rhetoric or Reality*, Bedford Square Press/NCVO, 1981.

This book describes a study of eight Councils of Voluntary Services (CVSs) and Rural Community Councils (RCCs). The authors' broad aims were to describe interaction at the local level between voluntary and statutory organisations and to discuss voluntary sector participation in social planning.

They saw the value context of their research as the pluralist approach to the planning and provision of welfare and community services advocated by the *Wolfenden Committee*. From this viewpoint, two major roles could be envisaged for intermediary voluntary bodies like CVSs and RCCs. They could have 'a change or development role' bringing new organisations into existence and encouraging existing ones; or they could have 'an integrative role', bringing together both individual voluntary organisations and the voluntary and statutory sectors in collaborative provision and planning.

In fact, though, the study found a very limited commitment in CVSs and RCCs to development and participation in policymaking. Limitations seemed be imposed by their multiple constituencies and goals; by their own lack of coherent organisational machinery for making effective decisions; and by the fact that they were able to gain credibility from the performance of other tasks such as the provision of information and administrative services.

As regards the integrative role of CVSs and RCCs, the author found that it also was limited. The policy and practice of local authorities was to view the voluntary sector as a 'valuable but less than equal' partner, so that collaboration was rarely possible. Individual voluntary organisations tended to have independent relationships with the local authorities and to ignore the intermediary bodies for this purpose. In any case, there were many tensions inherent in the claim of CVSs and RCCs to be representative of voluntary bodies; individual voluntary agencies were mainly concerned with their own special purposes and not with being co-ordinated or represented.

The authors conclude that structural and environmental features constrain CVSs and RCCs in their pursuit of the intermediary functions of change and development on the one hand, and integration and co-ordination on the other. In any case, development and co-ordination may in fact be incompatible aims. The consensus required for co-ordination and integration to work effectively may impede the execution of a development and change role.

There are few *empirical* studies of this kind focusing on the functions and organisation of British voluntary agencies. Although concerned mainly with intermediary rather than primary agencies, the study's findings about governing bodies, staff roles, the effect of funding sources, clarification of goals, and relationships with other agencies, echo findings of other studies of service-providing agencies (see, for example, *Hadley et al, 1975*, and *Kramer, 1981*).

M. H. Lenn, *A Study of the Role of Area Committees within the Family Welfare Association*, M.A. Dissertation, Brunel University, 1972.

The study reported in this dissertation was concerned with the relationship between the central (national) level of organisation in the Family Welfare Association and its local (or area) structures, especially its local committees.

The researcher found four main spheres of organisational confusion. These concerned relationships between central and area committees; between area committees and local paid officers; between area committees and central office paid officials; and between central and local paid officials. The study focused on the first two types of relationship.

M. Lenn, *The Outposted Volunteer: A Study of Working Relationships Between Voluntary and Statutory Services*, Volunteer Centre, 1982.

This booklet reports a research study of Marriage Guidance Counsellors outposted to five local health centres and seven Social Work Department offices in Scotland.

The author suggests that many of the problems which beset the outpostings 'appear to have arisen from a lack of clarification of important issues in the preparatory stages'. These issues included 'such questions as: who should be held accountable for work with the client; what should be the basis for referrals; who should handle the administrative arrangements; and what accommodation would be needed'.

Some issues of accountability were raised by the study. The outposted voluntary worker could be held accountable to both the host and the parent agency, so that the host was less able to exercise effective discipline. A second issue arose from the fact that volunteers working in statutory authorities could not be subject to managerial authority. As a result, neither they, nor the person who allocated work to them, seemed to be subject to public accountability. Lenn says that there are, perhaps, some tasks which for this reason should not be allocated to volunteers. Alternatively, where a 'volunteer is carrying out work for which

69

someone will be held accountable if it is carried out unsatisfactorily', an agreement of some kind should perhaps be signed which would focus the volunteer's attention on public accountability.

T. Levitt, *The Third Sector: New Tactics for a Responsive Society*, Allen and Unwin/AMACOM, New York, 1973.

Levitt was among the first writers to draw attention to the existence in the United States of a 'third sector' of activity comprising 'a residuum of public and private sectors'. This particular book is about the social policy implications for American society of some of the activities of third sector organisations.

J. Lissner, *Politics of Altruism: A Study of the Political Behaviour of Voluntary Development Agencies*, Lutheran World Federation, Geneva, 1977. (ILL)

Lissner describes his study as 'a systematic attempt to identify the political "laws of nature" which govern the behaviour and policy-making' of agencies directed towards Third World poverty.

Local Authorities Management Services and Computer Committee (LAMSAC), *Voluntary Action Westminster: Job Evaluation Kit*, LAMSAC, 1983.

This booklet is a guide to enable local voluntary organisations to decide on appropriate salaries for their paid staff. Factors which should be taken into account include education, supervisory responsibility, responsibility for assets, creative work and complexity of work. Suggested salaries are based on nationally agreed salary scales for local authority workers.

London Voluntary Services Council (LVSC), *Voluntary but not amateur: a guide to the law for voluntary organisations and community groups*, LVSC, 1980.

A. R. Longley, M. Dockray and J. Sallon, *Charity Trustees' Guide*, Bedford Square Press/NCVO, 1982 (2nd Edition).

This short booklet is a handbook 'for the preliminary guidance of those managing – or contemplating the management of – organisations established according to the law of England and Wales for charitable purposes'. It explains the meaning of charitable status and also the status, power and duties of trustees; the possible constitutional forms of charities; and the law relating to the taxation of charities.

Lovelock Report, *Review of the National Association of Citizens Advice Bureaux*, Cmnd. 9139, HMSO, 1984.

An enquiry chaired by Sir Douglas Lovelock was appointed by the Secretary of State for Trade in 1983 following expressions of concern about the impartiality of the CAB service. It was asked to review the functioning of the National Association of Citizens Advice Bureaux (NACAB) and 'to make recommendations with a view to ensuring that the Association offers the best possible service and support to local citizens advice bureaux', and that the monies available to NACAB which come entirely from central government, 'are spent in the most effective way'.

The report suggests that the decentralised, representative structure of the CAB service (in which each local bureau is autonomous and is represented at the national level through regional representatives) is appropriate and ensures that the service 'remains responsive to local needs and retains the loyalty and commitment of its volunteer workforce'. However, the authors argue that local management committees 'must recognise their financial responsibilities and take an active part in monitoring the operation of their bureaux', if the service is to continue to be 'effective and properly representative'.

An examination of the management structure of NACAB found 'a reluctance on the part of managers to exercise their authority and to assess relative costs and priorities'. Lines of responsibility were often not clearly defined. The report proposes changes in the managerial structure within NACAB and the strengthening of resources at the Area (regional) Office level.

The arrangements for funding the national and regional levels of the service and local bureaux are reviewed. 'Broadly speaking, bureaux are funded by local authorities and NACAB by Central Government, though NACAB chooses to pass roughly a quarter of its grant to bureaux.' The committee recommend that more funding should be channelled to local bureaux from central government but in a manner which will also encourage and preserve the principle of local authority funding for local bureaux.

As regards the aims and goals of CAB, the report agrees that attempts by the service to influence social policy are proper and useful, but it recommends that this should be ancillary to the goal of providing information and advice.

The Lovelock enquiry provides a unique opportunity for studying at first hand the nature of the relationship between central government and a major voluntary agency. The CAB service emerges as 'an invaluable national asset' but, nevertheless, it is shown to be not immune to some of the organisational problems which seem to characterise the voluntary sector.

C. C. Lundberg, 'Organisation Change in the Third Sector', *Public Administration Review*, September/October 1975, pp. 472–477.

Defining 'third sector' organisations as 'those occurring at the public/private interface', Lundberg presents a thesis of organisational change in the sector.

71

He draws on the writings of Lorsch and Lawrence* on differentiation and integration of authority within organisations, to argue that there is a pull in third sector organisations between bureaucracy and flexibility. A major dilemma is the 'need to keep the organization and its sub-systems sufficiently well coordinated without stunting adaptiveness'.

Lundberg argues that change strategies of third sector organisations build pressures for an 'openly-chosen structure'; a stage of 'organisational maturation' beyond that of a bureaucracy. However, there are also forces of resistance to change which may be especially prominent in third sector organisations. These forces include informal reward systems; lack of internal competence to bring about change; and highly visible decision-making processes which make for unstable power relationships. In addition, there is a tendency to respond to external pressures by bureaucratisation; that is, boundary rigidity, goal displacement, goal succession or goal modification.

* J. W. Lorsch and P. R. Lawrence (eds), *Studies in Organization Design*, Irwin, Homewood, Illinois, 1970.

M. McGill and L. Wooten (eds), 'A Symposium: Management in the Third Sector', *Public Administration Review*, September/October, 1975, pp. 433–477 (1).

This is a collection of articles by different writers about aspects of what is termed the 'third sector' in the United States; that is, all those institutions and organisations which are a part of neither the government sphere of activity, nor of the private, profit-directed sector. Voluntary agencies are a part of this third sector but the term encompasses also professional associations, trade unions, and quangos.

M. McGill and L. Wooten, 'Management in the Third Sector', *Public Administration Review*, September/October 1975, pp. 444–455 (2).

This article draws on a number of theoretical writings to discuss the types and distinctive features of third sector organisations.

The authors refer particularly to the work of *Frank* who contrasted two organisational models; one based on his own ideas about 'goal ambiguity' and the other derived from Weber's concept of rational bureaucracy. McGill and Wooten suggest that Frank's ambiguous goal model may be applicable to third sector organisations and the traditional Weberian model to public and private sector organisations. In third sector organisations, goal ambiguity may give rise to a behavioural pattern among managers which Frank described as 'conflicting standards of behaviour'. This is a major challenge to the effectiveness of third sector organisations generally.

Using Perrow's* analysis of goals in complex organisations, the authors then go on to argue that, among third sector organisations, it is not so much the voluntary organisations, administrative organisations or professional organisations which have high goal ambiguity. Rather it is the 'multiple organisations', such as NASA, for example, which are obliged to bring together many diverse functions, which display this characteristic.

* C. Perrow, 'The Analysis of Goals in Complex Organisations', *American Sociological Review*, April 1967, pp. 194–208.

The authors' conclusion that voluntary organisations do not have high goal ambiguity contrasts with the results of some empirical studies. *Hadley et al, 1975, Handy, 1981, James*, and *Leat et al, 1981*, for example, all found evidence of confusion about objectives and goals in voluntary agencies.

C. D. McKee, *Charitable Organisations*, Centre for Urban and Regional Studies, University of Birmingham, 1974.

This booklet reports on a survey of welfare and medical voluntary agencies conducted by the Department of Social Administration at Birmingham University in co-operation with a local review of charities. A total of 233 agencies were included in the study.

The functions of charitable organisations were analysed in three broad categories of direct service, indirect service (e.g. financial assistance to individuals, groups or other charities) and compound functions. Similarly, three kinds of organisational structure were discerned:

● charities administered solely by trustees
● charities administered by a committee with or without members
● 'diverse' structures with more than one constituted governing body.

An analysis of the goals of charities suggested that even when charities had diffuse manifest objectives, in practice, objectives were defined more narrowly, in line with trustees' own interests. Moreover, charities tended to be reluctant to support anything other than 'tried and tested causes with proven records of success'.

The author found deficiencies in co-operation between agencies. There was an insufficient flow of information between charities needing money and those providing grants and no focus to encourage or facilitate co-operation.

This is part of the small body of literature which focuses on the voluntary sector operating at the local level (see also *Hatch, 1980 (1), Newton*, and *Cousins, 1978*).

J. Maizels: see p. 54.

Manpower Services Commission (MSC), *Voluntary Organisations and the MSC Special Programmes*, MSC, Sheffield, 1982.

This booklet discusses the contribution to the MSC's Special Programmes of voluntary organisations and their possible roles in the future.

73

G. P. Marshall, 'The Control of Private Charities', *Public Administration*, 56, 3, 1978, pp. 343–352.

This article discusses 'the charity firm as seen from the economist's viewpoint' and also reviews the role of the Charity Commissioners in controlling charitable activity. The author argues that 'economic theory indicates that there may be forces at work which dull the incentive to seek maximum efficiency in the administration of charities'. For example, donors may not monitor the charity's governors, and governors in turn may not be very concerned about identifying appropriate beneficiaries. Economies of scale could be achieved by pooling of information and fund-raising efforts.

A monitoring agency such as the Charity Commissioners is needed, but there are problems in defining a charity and 'in establishing an appropriate model of efficiency for charitable institutions'.

MDU Bulletin

This bulletin first appeared in May 1983, and is published by the Management Development Unit of NCVO. There are three issues a year.

M. Meacher: see p. 31.

J. Mellett, 'Self-help, Mental Health and Professionals' in S. Hatch (ed), *Mutual Aid and Social and Health Care*, ARVAC/NCSS, 1980.

This paper discusses the possible ways in which self-help groups can use professionals' expertise without jeopardising their self-help nature.

I. Mocroft: see pp. 50; 51; 52 (two entries).

P. Montana: see p. 23.

P. Morgan-Jones: see p. 22.

R. Morris, 'Do Voluntaries Need Shaking Up?' *Castle Street Circular*, No. 100, Liverpool Council for Voluntary Service (CVS), 1978, pp. 3–4.

This article starts by pointing out the emphasis placed on good management in the voluntary sector by the *Wolfenden Committee 1978*: 'keeping up to date, monitoring performance, studying how far users and consumers are satisfied with what they receive'. The author goes on to discuss some of the obstacles to good management and planning in the voluntary sector. First, there is the heavy influence of external forces 'which produces fluctuations in income, involves outsiders in policy and makes research difficult'. A second obstacle is that technical skills and 'much of what is accepted as good management elsewhere' seems hostile to the participative spontaneous and flexible aspects of voluntary effort. The third obstacle is the difficulty of matching skills with requirements, especially in the smaller voluntary agencies.

The author argues that the Wolfenden Committee was right in saying that the quality of management and planning in the voluntary sector should be improved. Management skills are needed for survival in the face of financial and legal changes affecting voluntary bodies, and self-criticism is essential if a pioneer approach and a responsiveness to public needs is to be maintained.

S. Morrison, 'What is wrong with voluntary organisations?', *Social Service Quarterly*, 46, 1, July-September, 1972, pp. 9–11.

In this article, Sara Morrison argues that voluntary organisations should 'look in the mirror' and reassess features such as their declared aims, their priorities in spending resources, the best way to attract and support volunteers, and their relationship with statutory agencies.

C. L. Mulford and M. A. Mulford, 'Independence and Intra-organizational Structure for Voluntary Organizations', *Journal of Voluntary Action Research*, 9, 1–4, 1980, pp. 20–34.

This article examines the relationship between innovativeness in voluntary organisations and their interdependence with other agencies.

R. Mullin, *Present Alms: on the Corruption of Philanthropy*, Phlogiston Publishing, 1980.

The author's purpose in this booklet is to distinguish and discuss 'the distinctive features of philanthropy'. He argues that charities need greater opportunities for vigorous growth and development and that improvements are needed in the quality of governors, staff and volunteers. Charitable organisations 'must meet the demands for good stewardship and open accountability' which arise from the tax privileges and donations they receive and from the powerless of the needy whom they serve.

A chapter entitled 'The Charities Themselves' analyses the responsibilities of charitable governing bodies and notes that, in recruiting governors, public standing is not as important as skills, knowledge, commitment and a disinterested outlook. Staff must be remunerated 'reasonably' and must be given the training and career development which will help their agencies and facilitate staff mobility between agencies.

The author argues strongly that what is needed is 'good and creative people' and the resources to help and support them in individual agencies, rather than a strengthening of 'voluntary bureaucracies, the intermediary bodies in *Wolfenden*'s terminology'.

G. J. Murray, 'Voluntary Organisations in the Personal Social Services Field', in W. F. Maunder (ed), *Reviews of U.K. Statistical Sources, Vol. I*, Heinemann, 1974.

Although the figures are now outdated, this article provides a useful reference review of sources of statistics about voluntary organisations.

G. J. Murray, *Voluntary Organisations and Social Welfare: An Administrator's Impressions*, Oliver and Boyd, 1969.

The aim of the study reported in this book was to provide some perspectives of voluntary organisations. The author looked at their individual organisational characteristics; their relationships with each other; their impact on central and local government; and their place 'as part of national activities'. The focus was on social welfare voluntary agencies in Scotland.

A chapter on organisation concentrates on discussing national headquarters structures and major coordinating organisations. It draws attention to the lack of management staff in voluntary agencies and the detrimental effect of this on developmental work as against day-to-day administration. The author also discusses the problem of achieving a governing body or council which is adequately representative of members and other interests but which is also of a size and composition suited to effective decision-making.

N. Murray, 'The Travails of Task Force', *Voluntary Action*, Autumn 1981, pp. 10–12.

This article discusses the major dispute between staff and the Board of Management of Task Force which occurred in 1981. It summarises the early history of Task Force and traces the changes that occurred in the agency's approach to volunteers and to the elderly whom the agency was set up to serve.

The views of various people about the factors precipitating the 1981 dispute are presented. They all tend to focus on the staff's commitment to participative and non-hierarchical management forms and related problems of control by the governing body and accountability for funds and services.

N. Murray, 'Is the Charity Law an Ass?', *Community Care*, 7 October 1982, pp. 12–14.

This article discusses the constraints placed on the activities of individual charities by the provisions of existing charity law.

National Federation of Community Organisations (NFCO), *Guidelines for Local Federal Organisations,* **NFCO, 1982.**

This is a collection of documents supplied in a loose-leaf folder relating to the promotion and running of local community associations.

National Federation of Housing Associations (NFHA), *Growing Pains: Coping with the Problems of Growth in Housing Associations,* **NFHA, 1978.**

This booklet was compiled by an NFHA Working Party and is intended primarily as a guide for housing associations with between 50 and 500 homes, going through the first major stage of growth. It deals with organisational growth from the stage when it is no longer possible for committees, staff and tenants to handle issues on an *ad hoc* basis; decisions have to be formally stated.

The report distinguishes three kinds of potential problems arising from growth. First, there are those related directly to clients' needs, including criteria for selection of tenants, communication with tenants, and day-to-day management. Second, there may be problems internal to the association, relating, for example, to office administration, staffing, control and development of the committee of management. In all of these cases, procedures and structures may outgrow the original purposes and the capabilities of original role-holders. Third, there may be problems in relation to other organisations and individuals in the area.

The report makes several practical suggestions for dealing with each of the potential problems. For example, in relation to staffing problems arising from growth, for example, the report suggests planning ahead before breaking point is reached; issuing job descriptions to give a wider knowledge and understanding of staff functions; a formal training programme; staff performance assessments to ensure that jobs remain within individual capabilities; and clear staff structures either by functional divisions or in multi-discipline teams. As regards management committees, the report points to the need for clearly defined and allocated functions; regular reviews of membership; and clear delegation of executive action to the staff.

The organisational problems arising from growth in the voluntary sector have been noted elsewhere (see, for example, *Chapin and Tsouderos, Hadley et al,* 1975, *Hyman,* and *Jerman*). But ways of tackling the problem have been little discussed. Although this booklet is addressed to practitioners in housing associations it is likely to be of wider interest.

NCVO Legal Department, *'Legal Responsibilities of Members of Committees of Unincorporated Voluntary Organisations',* **Guidance Note 1, NCVO, 1981.**

NCVO Legal Department, '*Charities: Constitutional Forms and Liabilities of Trustees*', Guidance Note 2, NCVO, 1981.

This five-page note provides a clear summary of the basic types of constitution which may be adopted for a charity. It goes on to explain the 'nature and extent of the potential personal liability' of managing or charity trustees.

NCVO, *Action for Social Progress – The United Kingdom Experience*, NCVO, 1982.

This booklet deals with the responsibilities of governmental and voluntary agencies in specific service and policy areas. It was prepared by the U.K. International Committee of the International Council on Social Welfare (ICSW) for the 21st International Conference of ICSW in 1982. (See *Scott, 1982*, for the *World Report* on this and other contributions.)

The U.K. document includes contributions from a variety of voluntary organisations operating broadly in the social welfare field, on how voluntary and statutory agencies work together for their particular client groups.

NCVO Policy Analysis Unit, *The Management and Effectiveness of Voluntary Organisations*, NCVO, 1984.

This booklet is the report of a small working group which was invited by NCVO 'to define the management and organisational issues raised for voluntary organisations' when their income derives largely from central or local government.

The report distinguishes five problem areas underlying confusion about the state-voluntary sector partnership:

- Muddled beginnings to the relationship, with no clear statements about objectives or expectations.
- Insecurity caused by short-term funding and changes in funders' programmes.
- Problems of financial accountability.
- Inadequate review and evaluation procedures.
- Political friction caused by different perceptions of what constitutes acceptable 'political' activity by voluntary agencies.

Taking each area in turn, the report considers the issues and recommends some desirable changes. It suggests, for example, that a distinction be made between funding to support the general objectives of a voluntary organisation (in which case 'arm's length' agreements should be made between funders and agencies), and funds which 'buy a specific service in pursuit of government objectives'. In the latter case a specific contract is called for. As regards financial accountability and evaluation procedures, the report emphasises the need for voluntary agencies to be encouraged to develop their own expertise and resources in these fields.

78

The NCVO's 'Code for Voluntary Organisations' on 'Relations between the Voluntary Sector and Government' is appended to the booklet.

This report develops and broadens the discussion by the *Association of Metropolitan Authorities, etc.* It clarifies the areas which are sources of confusion in the statutory/voluntary relationship and makes some practical suggestions about changes that voluntary agencies can make in their own procedures when handling statutory funding.

NCVO: see also p. 15 and p. 77.

W. H. Newman and H. W. Wallender, 'Managing Not-for-Profit Enterprises', *Academy of Management Review***, 3, January 1978, pp. 24–31.**

This article discusses whether business management principles can be applied to the non-profit sector. It suggests that although the processes of management may be the same in all enterprises, it may not always be appropriate to execute them in the same way.

K. Newton, *Second City Politics***, Oxford University Press, 1976.**

This book reports a study of the local political system in Birmingham. The 'political activity rates' of formally-organised voluntary associations are examined.

W. E. Nielsen, *The Endangered Sector***, Columbia University Press, New York, 1979.**

In this book, Nielsen attempts to construct some tentative theories from 'the patchwork of evidence' available about non-profit organisations. However, he specifically omits from consideration private social welfare agencies (which includes voluntary agencies) because he regards them as too numerous and diverse.

B. Nightingale, *Charities***, Allen Lane, 1973.**

This book is a popular account of the British charities scene. It describes the functions and activities of charities and discusses aspects of fund-raising and future trends.

M. Norton, *A Guide to the Benefits of Charitable Status***, Directory of Social Change, 1982.**

H. Orlans (ed), *Nonprofit Organizations: A Government Management Tool*, **Praeger Publications, New York, 1980.**

Orlans has collected together in this book a series of conference papers on the way in which the United States government contracts work, especially social demonstration projects. The focus of the paper is on public policy rather than on the implications of contracting for the organisations themselves. (This latter viewpoint is discussed, for example, in *Hartogs and Weber, 1978*, and *Judge*.)

J. Pawsey, *The Tringo Phenomenon*, **Adam Smith Institute, 1983.**

This booklet draws attention to the existence of what the author describes as 'TRINGOS' – Tax-Receiving Independent Non-Government Organisations. Many charities and voluntary agencies are TRINGOS.

The author is concerned that public funds are not necessarily being spent in a reasonable way and on 'worthy' purposes in supporting TRINGOS. He urges co-ordination between government ministries allocating grants, and more accountability to the House of Commons. Recurrent grants should not be given automatically and voluntary contributions should be encouraged through 'matching' funding schemes.

J. L. Pearce, 'Apathy or Self-Interest? The Volunteer's Avoidance of Leadership Roles', *Journal of Voluntary Action Research*, **9, 1–4, 1980, pp. 85–94.**

This article focuses on the leadership role in voluntary associations and organisations.

The study described drew data from some all-volunteer social service organisations matched with seven all-employee-run-and-staffed organisations with similar primary tasks. It was found that volunteers are much less likely than employees to pursue positions of leadership.

The author argues that volunteers are not lacking in feeling or commitment. Their inactivity is explained by the fact that, unlike employees, they do not receive perquisites from leadership apart from the ability to influence organisational policy. On the contrary, they must 'normally expend even greater amounts of their free time in the service of the organization's goals'.

J. R. Pennock and J. W. Chapman (eds), *Voluntary Associations*, **Nomos, XI, Atherton Press, New York, 1969.**

This series of discussion papers is concerned with political and legal theories relevant to the existence and activities of voluntary associations.

A. Phillips with K. Smith, *Charitable Status: A Practical Handbook*, Inter-Action, 1982. (Books published by Inter-Action are now available from Inter Change, 15 Wilkin Street, London NW5 3NG, or via Turnaround Books Distributors.)

This book is a clearly-explained guide to the law of charity including material on legal formats, charity trusteeship, political campaigning, covenants and tax relief.

A. Pike, 'The Big Business Side of Charity', *Financial Times*, 8 December 1982, p. 12.

This article describes the growth over the last 30 years of the Spastics Society which now generates more than £22m a year and has over 2,400 staff. The changes in management structure instituted by Tim Yeo when he became Director in 1980 are listed. 'One of the most radical changes was that the Society's 15-strong elected executive council of lay representatives should be concerned only with policy issues.' Management and administration was the responsibility of a management board which consisted of 12 senior members of the staff and the elected council. Committees were given only advisory functions.

D. Pitt Francis: see p. 99.

J. Posnett: see p. 16.

C. Quine and J. Bazalgette, *The Role of the Young Volunteer*, Final Report on a Pilot Project Funded by SSRC, Grubb Institute, 1979.

This study of mobilisation of young volunteers by four voluntary agencies includes an examination of forms of organisation and leadership used by the different agencies.

M. Rankin: see p. 24.

M. Rein, 'The Transition from Social Movement to Organization', in W. A. Glaser and D. L. Sills (eds), *The Government of Associations*, Bedminster Press, Totowa, New Jersey, 1966. (ILL)

This paper describes the Planned Parenthood Federation of America which began as a social movement advocating contraception. It later changed its goals in response to changed needs and attitudes and became concerned with planned families and world population.

D. Reith, 'Organisation in the Social Services. A Comparison Between Local Authority Departments and Voluntary Agencies', in J. Lishman (ed), *Social Work Departments as Organisations*, Research Highlights No. 4, Department of Social Work, University of Aberdeen, 1982.

Drawing on his personal impressions of large, national voluntary agencies, the author of this article outlines some broad organisational differences between local authority social work departments in Scotland and voluntary agencies which employ paid staff.

R. M. Rice, 'Impact of Government Contracts on Voluntary Social Agencies', *Social Casework*, 56, July 1975, pp. 387–395.

The main contention in this article is 'that the hidden incentives contained in governmental financing of voluntary services may constrict the independence' of voluntary social agencies.

During the 1960s, many social service agencies were founded in the United States 'using the usual structure of voluntarism', but, the author argues, these were not true community developments. They were rather a response to legislation and an instrument for executing government policy. In these new kinds of voluntary agencies the tension between values of independence and accountability are acute. This is especially so because their boards of directors tend to be less close to agency operations and accountability procedures. They therefore tend to depend less on good faith and more on sets of rules that maintain strong central policy direction over the apparatus of the voluntary institutions.

Government funding – whether in the form of lump-sum grants, programme contracts or purchase of service contracts – tends to pressure voluntary agencies to innovate and increase the quantity of services favoured by government. They are discouraged from independent thinking about social problems. Private subsidies are given to implement government goals.

Several North American writers have been concerned with the implications for the management of voluntary agencies of new and increasing governmental funding (see comment on *Rosenbaum*).

A. Richardson and M. Goodman, *Self-Help and Social Care: Mutual Aid Organisations in Practice*, Policy Studies Institute, 1983.

This book reports a study of self-help groups sponsored by the DHSS and carried out by the Policy Studies Institute. Four national self-help groups and their branches were studied through questionnaires and interviews: MENCAP; the National Association of Widows; Gingerbread; and the National Council for the Single Woman and Her Dependents. The study focused on groups at local level, several of which undertook large projects with paid staff.

The authors found that, although groups generally made a significant contribution to the welfare of their local communities, their ability to provide extensive services for their members was limited. Moreover, membership of self-help groups was often apathetic, with a high turnover.

Ways in which local groups may be fostered and supported are suggested and the positive role of paid staff, both at national and local level, are noted in the study.

Although the precise headquarters structures varied between the four national groups, 'the nature of central-local relations did not differ strikingly between the separate organisations. In no case were they wholly easy.' As part of their analysis the authors suggest alternative models.

Although primarily concerned with self-help groups, this study contains much material of interest for what the authors call the more 'traditional' type of voluntary agency. The work is an important contribution to the literature which examines the interface between informal and formal care (*Abrams*, *1981 (1)*).

The approach of the authors is also significant in that they attempt to link the practical problems facing individuals and groups to the implications for social policy (*Billis*, *1984 (1)*).

D. Robinson and S. Henry, 'Alcoholics Anonymous in England and Wales: Basic Results from a Survey', *British Journal on Alcohol and Alcoholism***, 13, 1978, pp. 36–44.**

This article reports the results of a 1976 survey of members of Alcoholics Anonymous and gives a profile of current membership.

F. Robinson and S. Robinson, *Neighbourhood Care: An Exploratory Bibliograpy***, Volunteer Centre, 1982.**

This bibliography contains 143 entries, with commentary, on the theme of neighbourhood care. Special reference is made to locally-based volunteer projects.

J. Robinson: see p. 40.

A. Rogers: see p. 14.

N. Rosenbaum, 'Government Funding and the Voluntary Sector: Impacts and Options', *Journal of Voluntary Action Research***, 10, 1, January-March, 1981, pp. 82–89.**

This article discusses the management and governance impacts on the U.S. voluntary sector which have arisen from the recent 'greatly expanded intercourse between government and voluntary institutions'.

The author argues that increased funding has accelerated the trend towards bureaucratisation in voluntary agencies and has led to dominance of administrative over substantive work. Boards of management feel distant from government-funded programmes and staff views are therefore able to predominate. Community involvement in the form of fund-raising and volunteering declines with government funding so that agencies are separated from the grassroots and obliged to seek ever more government support.

The author suggests changes in government policy, including more channelling of funds through intermediary agencies. He also advocates that agencies do some of their own fund-raising and involve their clientele in governance and evaluation. Suggested changes in voluntary sector policy and practice include the establishment of 'administrative services consortia' to provide necessary professional services and refusal of grants with overly-burdensome bureaucratic requirements. 'Collective assertiveness' by voluntary agencies towards government is necessary and boards of directors should only accept government programmes which are 'compatible with the central mission of the organisation'.

The organisational implications for voluntary agencies of statutory funding in various forms is a frequent theme in the North American literature. Several writers focus, like Rosenbaum, on effects on agencies' *goals* and on the problems of managing and being *accountable* for money provided (see, for example, *Rice*, *Berg and Wright*, and *Hartogs and Weber, 1978*). Whereas *Kramer, 1979 (2)* and *Hartogs and Weber*, 1978, suggest that government funds are not inherently corrupting to agency goals, *Rosenbaum*, like *Rice* and *Sharkansky*, sounds notes of caution.

Practical suggestions as to how voluntary agencies may avoid some of the disadvantages of government funding are also given by *Hartogs and Weber, 1978*. *Judge* and *Utting* have attempted to relate United States experience of government funding to Britain.

A. Rowe, 'Participation and the Voluntary Sector: The Independent Contribution', *Journal of Social Policy*, 7, 1, 1978, pp. 41–56.

The author states that his aim in this article is to create a general theoretical model for the voluntary sector, using participation as a central concept.

He discusses three possible ways of classifying voluntary organisations: according to the functional divisions used by governmental agencies; on a scale ranging from self-help to altruism; or according to who might participate in them and to whom they should be accountable.

As regards participation, Rowe suggests that, in fact, there is very little real participation in the voluntary sector and that many charitable trusts are elitist. As regards other voluntary organisations, pressures of time and expertise tend to push control into the hands of people who do a job for others.

Rowe proposes a theoretical model of two types of voluntary organisations, Type A and Type B. Voluntary organisations of Type A are self-help in aim and key decisions are made by client-members. Their main functions are mutual contact and support and there is participatory, democratic involvement by consumers. The aim of Type B organisations is altruism, and key decisions are made by executive staff and honorary committees. They regard their main function as the provision of an efficient service to clients. Consumers do not directly participate in the organisation; at best, there is representative democracy, consumer research and some complaints machinery.

Public authorities, favour financing Type B organisations, as these are more obviously 'accountable'. This encourages voluntary organisations to 'act responsibly' and cling to their elitist management system. But, in fact, organisations with a higher degree of consumer participation may be *more* responsive, flexible and cost-effective than more traditionally organised ones. The voluntary sector's unique contribution should now be not so much in trying out new activities – this can be done by statutory authorities – but in making participation work.

Most writers concerned with the issue of *accountability* in the voluntary sector have focused on external aspects, the means by which voluntary agencies can be made responsive to funders, clients and the public at large (for example, *Judge*, *Hatch and Mocroft*, *1983*, and *Austin and Posnett*). In this paper, Rowe has widened the discussion of accountability by drawing in some internal organisational characteristics, such as governing bodies and participation by members.

J. E. Ruckle, *Distinctive Qualities of Third Sector Organizations*, University of California, PhD Dissertation, 1981. (Copies obtainable from The Micrographics Dept., Doheny Library, University of Southern California, Los Angeles, CA 9007.)

Two questions provide the focus for this study: 'are there distinguishable qualities which characterise the third sector?' and 'what implications do the distinctive qualities of the third sector have for public policy and for improving the management of these organisations?' Ruckle examined the questions using existing writings about the third sector as well as some empirical data of his own derived from interviews with participants in third sector organisations.

Defining 'third-sector organisations' as those 'at the public/private interface', which are neither strictly private business enterprises not purely governmental bodies, Ruckle points out that the sector comprises a wide variety of organisations. These include not only voluntary associations but also not-for-profit organisations, professional associations, quasi-public organisations, trade unions, religious organisations, trans-organisational clusters, universities and others.

Ruckle analysed his data about third-sector organisations in terms of three dimensions; the formational dimension, comprising the organisational philosophy and structure; the contextural dimension, which includes the relationship between the organisation and its environment; and resource management, the way in which human and material resources are used in the organisation. He found that third-sector organisations provide vehicles for the expression of values independent of the profit concerns of business and the prevailing political priorities of government. The voluntary governing board is a distinctive structural attribute and the character of member involvement differs from that of the private and public sectors. Third-sector organisations, he argues, have a high innovation potential because they are less subject to control and 'bureau-pathology'. Distinctive features of resource management in the third sector include the use of volunteers; the psychic rewards available to employees; the multiple and diverse expectations of participants; and significant charitable contributions.

Ruckle concludes that organisation theory and the 'prevailing bureaucratic paradigm' in particular, is too generalised to be applied to third-sector organisations, which have such distinctive features. He believes that effectiveness in the third sector could be improved by special training; more use of voluntary resources; alternative forms of funding; and new management incentive systems.

Ruckle's thesis brings together two questions which have generally been separately considered in other literature.

Firstly, 'does the voluntary sector have distinctive organisational features?' (for example, *Kramer, 1981*) and secondly, 'How far can management techniques and organisational theory developed in other arenas be applied to the voluntary sector?' (for example, *Snell* and *Gerard, 1983*).

J. Sallon: see p. 70.

D. Scott, *Don't Mourn for Me. . . . Organise: The Social and Political Uses of Voluntary Organisations*, Allen and Unwin, Sydney, 1981.

This book provides an over-view of the role of the voluntary sector in welfare provision in Australia.

D. Scott, *World Report for the Twenty-first International Conference on Social Welfare: Action for Social Progress – The Responsibilities of Government and Voluntary Organisations*, **International Council on Social Welfare, Austria, 1982. (Copies obtainable from NCVO.)**

This pamphlet is an annotated report compiled from completed questionnaires returned from members of the International Council on Social Welfare (ICSW) about the voluntary sector in their countries. It also includes the views of international member organisations.

Scott notes the underpinning values for voluntary organisations as freedom of association; freedom of expression; pluralism; and participation in decision-making. Governments turn to the voluntary sector because of the desire to fulfil community obligations and/or to cut back in their own spending and get resulting 'gaps' filled.

The information obtained from ICSW members about functions of voluntary organisations was analysed using Kramer's typology of functions; namely, vanguard, advocate or watchdog, service-provider and value-guardian (*Kramer, 1981*). Service-provision probably occupies 95 per cent of the time and resources of voluntary organisations in all countries. 'In the economically less-developed and industrialised countries voluntary organisations are preoccupied with basic needs. In countries where a reasonable level of income security exists, services are more concerned with personal adjustment and facilitating access to government health, housing and welfare services.' The advocacy function of voluntary organisations seems to be 'accepted more in principle than in practice'. This is not only because of the tendency to concentrate on service-provision but also because of the fear of being political, the lack of radical drive, and ignorance of the necessary techniques.

As regards the relations between voluntary organisations and government, these may consist of supplementing by voluntary organisations, or roles may be complementary or functions may be delegated by government to voluntary organisations. 'Few countries reported that government included representatives of voluntary organisations in national planning and decision-making relating to broad social policy, but there were more reports of voluntary representaton on advisory and consultative groups concerned with particular problems.'

Two problems emerged in connection with the relations between government and voluntary organisations. First, it was pointed out that close relations between the government and voluntary sectors may not be in the best interest of consumers. Second, it seems that in many countries government funds were attracted to areas with better voluntary administrative machinery, even though these areas were often in relatively less need.

Some fundamental questions for voluntary agencies about purposes, accountability, efficiency, effectiveness and participation are listed and the need for continuous self-evaluation is emphasised. 'While government and their public servants are subject to criticism, voluntary organisations are often seen to be beyond criticism. They are regarded as private bodies, or it is assumed that they are run by "good people doing good work"'.

This report contributes to the limited literature which draws on the experience of voluntary sector activity in several countries (see also *Kramer, 1981*, and *Lissner*). The common concern about the implications of a close relationship between government and voluntary agencies also appears in British writings by, for example, *Rowe, Cousins, 1978*, and *Smith and Hague*. The findings about the imbalance between advocacy and service-providing functions in voluntary sectors may be compared with the recommendations of the *Lovelock* enquiry.

The U.K. contribution to this document was published by NCVO, 1982.

Scottish Voluntary Organisations Group, *Voluntary Organisations: The Crisis Now*, Report of a Working Party, Scottish Council of Social Services, 1980. (ILL)

This report highlights the crisis facing Scottish voluntary agencies as a result of financial constraints and wider pressures to take on tasks and volunteers. It argues that government must have realistic expectations and must clearly understand the respective roles of the voluntary and statutory sectors. Examples are given of innovations by and workloads of voluntary agencies.

H. Search, 'Conflict in Charities' in B. Knight (ed), *Management in Voluntary Organisations*, Occasional Paper No. 6, ARVAC, Wivenhoe, Essex, 1984.

This paper describes research which examined 'the causes, manifestations and resolution of conflict' between paid employees of charities and their governing body. The author shows that the basis for conflict exists in struggles over rewards, duplication of functions, and differing norms and priorities. She hypothesises that conflict can be minimised where management committee and staff share a common culture and where 'a favourable attitude to the role of paid staff exists on the part of the committee'.

A. Sears: see p. 31.

S. Selwyn, (Edited by S. Humble), *Research into Voluntary Action 1977–80: A Directory*, Volunteer Centre, 1981.

This directory gives details about 306 projects which concentrate on, or touch on, volunteering activities in England, Wales, Scotland and Northern Ireland. It includes projects concerned with aspects of voluntary organisations.

J. M. Senor, 'Another Look at the Executive-Board Relationship', *Social Work*, 8, 2, April 1963, pp. 19–25.

This paper examines the nature of the relationship between Boards of Directors (governing bodies) and (paid) Executive Directors of non-governmental social work agencies in the United States. It argues that, in theory and in reality, this relationship is not a partnership, as is often supposed.

In theory, the Executive Director is subordinate to the Board which employs him or her and makes the policy which he or she carries out. In practice, the Executive Director may be superordinate to the Board.

The article examines some of the characteristics of the Board and of the agency that tend to increase the power of the Executive Director at the expense of the Board. As regards characteristics of the agency, the position of Board members will be relatively weak if they are physically and socially isolated from the work of the agency and reliant on staff for information; this is particularly likely to happen when the agency is running total institutions, such as residential homes. The paid Director may also become dominant where his staff are professionals engaged in highly technical or specialist work. In such cases the Executive Director totally controls the channels of communication between staff and clients on the one hand, and Boards on the other.

Characteristics of the Board itself may also strengthen the relative position of the paid Director, if for example, there is 'latent role conflict' among members, they will not act as a coherent group. Again, if Board members are motivated by the desire for individual rewards and distinctions, the Executive Director will hold 'a pivotal position of power'.

The nature of the relationship between governing bodies and staff has been described by several writers (for example *Kramer*, *1965*, *Harris*, and *Gouldner*). Senor moves beyond description and suggests some organisational features which might explain various kinds of relationship.

P. Seyd, 'Shelter: The National Campaign for the Homeless', *Political Quarterly*, 46, 4, 1975, pp. 418–431.

This article is primarily concerned with the impact of the activities of Shelter on the political debate about poverty in the 1960s and 70s.

The organisation started with fund-raising to promote re-housing activities and later moved to pressure-group activity stressing the idea of solutions to housing problems coming through governmental actions.

The author describes the problems of structure and organisation which arose when Shelter moved away from fund-raising and service-provision towards pressure-group activities. It was unclear who should or could 'speak for Shelter' and on whose behalf, since neither the homeless nor individual Shelter supporters played any significant part in the structure. The trustees were self-appointed and self-perpetuating and their relationship with staff and donors in the country was 'remote'. This 'benevolent paternalism' was later modified to some extent by the appointment of donor and staff representatives to the management committee.

P. Seyd, 'The Child Poverty Action Group', *Political Quarterly*, 47, 2, 1976, pp. 189–202.

This article provides an account of the development of the Child Poverty Action Group and its influence on, and involvement in, public policy-making.

I. Sharkansky, 'Policy-making and Service Delivery on the Margins of Government: The Case of Contractors', *Public Administration Review,* **March-April 1980, pp. 116–123.**

This article discusses the status and functions of the private and voluntary agencies which carry out tasks, including the provision of welfare services, for the United States government on a contract basis. Being largely self-governing, such bodies are not subject to the devices of political control which apply to government departments; and yet their inherent flexibility provides them with opportunities for doing both good and bad.

Voluntary agencies' involvement in government contracts may benefit clients by providing diversity and choice in service delivery. However, many dilemmas are raised. There are problems of co-ordination between agencies dealing with similar services. Government control and funding may dilute the autonomy and voluntarism for which voluntary agencies are valued and yet there may also be concern about the lack of public control over the programmes of voluntary agencies.

B. Shenfield and I. Allen, *The Organisation of Voluntary Service: A study of domiciliary visiting of the elderly by volunteers,* **PEP Broadsheet 533, Political and Economic Planning, 1972. (Obtainable from Policy Studies Institute.)**

The authors of this booklet interviewed 126 elderly people and 100 of their volunteer visitors. Much of the visiting was found to be inappropriate to the needs of individual elderly people.

The authors suggest that a scheme of regular, unhurried voluntary home-visiting presents complex organisational problems. A large number of volunteers dispersed in the field have to be controlled and deployed economically. Good procedures are needed for systematically locating and assessing those who would benefit from visiting, and for matching volunteers to the elderly. Volunteers need continuing support and advice if they are to remain after recruitment and maintain regular visiting.

The organisational structures of the bodies providing visiting services were inadequate in these respects. There was found to be a lack of staff and other resources; confusion about objectives; no feedback procedure; and no locally-based procedures for locating suitable clients.

This study pre-dates the more extensive study of Task Force (*Hadley et al, 1975*) but it is noteworthy that both studies found that the sources of inadequacies in volunteer visiting schemes were frequently organisational.

The importance of matching client needs to available volunteer resources and the need for an organisational framework for successful volunteer schemes is highlighted in *Abrams et al, 1981*.

V. M. Sieder, 'The Historical Origins of the American Volunteer', in W. A. Glaser and D. L. Sills (eds), *The Government of Associations*, Bedminster Press, Totowa, New Jersey, 1966. (ILL)

This article describes how the history of voluntary associations 'of the social service type' (i.e. voluntary social welfare agencies) in the United States has been affected by the evolution of American society. New societal problems have given rise to new organisations or goals or changes in existing ones. With the disappearance of a leisure-class, leadership has been professionalised.

D. Sills, *The Volunteers: Means and Ends in a National Organisation*, Free Press, Glencoe, Illinois, 1957.

Sills' classic sociological analysis of the National Foundation for Infantile Paralysis continues to provide a valuable case study of the processes of institutionalisation and bureaucratisation in a voluntary agency and the influence of an organisation's membership upon its fundamental character. The book discusses goal displacement and goal succession in voluntary agencies and the findings of the study are related to the conclusions of other studies of large-scale organisations.

D. L. Sills, 'Goal Succession in Four Voluntary Associations', in W. A. Glaser and D. L. Sills (eds), *The Government of Associations*, Bedminster Press, Totowa, New Jersey, 1966. (ILL)

This article follows the theme of 'goal succession' discussed in Sills' earlier study of the National Foundation for Infantile Paralysis (*D. Sills, 1957*). Four examples of adaptation to change by voluntary agencies are discussed.

The Woman's Christian Temperance Union failed to adjust its goals to changed circumstances and a second organisation, the Townsend Organisation, achieved its original goal but did not adopt a new one. Both organisations therefore declined. The two other agencies discussed – the YMCA and the American National Red Cross – did change their goals and methods to meet changed circumstances and therefore continued to flourish.

D. L. Sills: see also p. 37.

P. Sills, 'Voluntary Initiative and Statutory Reaction: A Study in the Political Control of Social Reform', *Community Development Journal*, 11, 2, 1976, pp. 120–125.

This article provides a case study of an initiative by a local voluntary group for housing single homeless people.

The response to the initiative by the local authority moved through seven stages: indifference; indecision; approval on trial; growth of opposition; dissension and arbitration. Finally the local authority moved to 'takeover and control by incorporation'.

The author concludes that local authorities want local groups to help them in the provision of services for which there is an established demand.

P. Sills, H. Butcher, P. Collis and A. Glen, 'The Formation and Forms of Community Groups', *Journal of Voluntary Action Research,* **9, 1980, pp. 189–202.**

This article draws on the study described in *Butcher et al, 1980*, to develop some hypotheses about the formation and development of community groups.

P. Sills: see also p. 24.

D. Sims: see p. 94 and p. 95.

B. L. R. Smith (ed), *The New Political Economy,* **Macmillan, 1975.**

This book derived from the same initiative of the Carnegie Corporation as the earlier volume (*Smith and Hague (eds), 1971*). The editor describes it as an exercise in political theory which 'explores the complex interrelations between government and other institutions participating in the policy process'. The primary focus is on those institutions which are highly professionalised and in receipt of substantial public funds. How are they to be made responsible to the people and to their traditional governmental representatives?

B. L. R. Smith and D. C. Hague (eds), *The Dilemma of Accountability in Modern Government,* **St Martin's Press, New York, 1971.**

This volume comprises a collection of papers written for a meeting which took place in England in 1969, of two parallel study groups in the United States and the United Kingdom. The study groups were sponsored by the Carnegie Corporation of New York (see also *B. Smith (ed), 1975*) and were concerned with the issues of independence and control inherent in the relationship between government and those contracted to do work with public funds.

Most of the papers are case studies of contracting for services by government in the two countries. Two introductory essays by the editors clarify some of the surrounding issues. Smith argues that the problem of accountability and independence in the 'contract state' can be broadly stated 'as the need to create the understandings and institutional arrangements that will enable the governments . . . to maintain a strong central policy direction over the apparatus of private institutions performing services for the government, while giving the private

92

institutions enough independence of operation to produce the maximum incentives for a distinctive and creative contribution to government'.

In his introductory essay, Hague suggests that 'independence' and 'control' must be regarded as key elements in accountability, with the tension between the two removed for the individual by the giving of a contract which specifies the authority delegated. He also suggests two aspects of accountability must be considered – accountability within the contractor's operations and within the system set up to ensure accountability.

C. Smith and A. Freedman, *Voluntary Associations: Perspectives on the Literature*, Harvard University Press, Cambridge, Mass., 1972. (ILL)

This book provides an account of the sociological and political theory literature relevant to the study of voluntary associations. The authors explain that the material is not organised into a 'theoretically-oriented propositional inventory' because the field of study is not yet sufficiently developed to permit this. Voluntary associations are defined as organisations which 'people belong to part-time and without pay such as clubs, lodges, good-works agencies and the like'. They are non-profit, non-government, private groups which are formally organised.

The authors point out that there is very little theory in the field of voluntary associations; only a series of unrelated hypotheses. Various typologies have been suggested using prime variables which include size, internal political structure, independence of outside control, societal functions, source of support, location, members' characteristics, beneficiaries, and whether they are instrumental or expressive.

Several chapters in the book are devoted to a discussion of the literature on pluralism and participation in political and social systems. The final chapter draws attention to some contemporary developments which raise sociological, organisational and policy issues; these include the blurring of the line between private voluntary action and governmental activity, the professionalisation and bureaucratisation of voluntary associations; problems of oligarchy; and the tendency to romanticise voluntarism.

D. H. Smith, 'Altruism, Volunteers and Volunteerism', *Journal of Voluntary Action Research*, 10, 1, January-March 1981, pp. 21–36.

After reviewing the extent to which volunteering is motivated by altruism, Smith discusses the differences between paid-staff non-profit organisations and volunteer non-profit organisations. He suggests that, whereas paid staff may have 'some significant altruism at the root of their quasi-volunteerism', volunteers have very little altruism in their motivations; 'material and solidary incentives' are more important to volunteers than altruistic attachment to the agency's goals.

G. Smith, *Social Work and the Sociology of Organisations*, especially Chapter 11, 'Voluntary Organisations', Routledge and Kegan Paul, 1979 (Revised Edition).

The focus of this short book is the sociology of social work organisations. The author's approach is to take existing organisations as they are and examine the 'limitations imposed on them by their organisational settings'. The final chapter takes some of the concepts and theories discussed in the book and explores their applicability to voluntary organisations. Voluntary organisations are defined, for the purposes of the chapter, as 'that loose grouping of organisations which are concerned to use the efforts of voluntary workers in the provision of social and community services'.

Smith argues that for a number of reasons, voluntary service organisations present acute leadership problems. This is partly because the absence of a formal authority structure prevents the disciplining of participants. It may also be because people within the organisation have differing perceptions of the organisation's structure and purposes. Voluntary service organisations share, in addition, the problem of control experienced in other organisations in which the locus of much initiative rests with 'front-line units', in this case, with volunteers and local groups. The response to these problems of leadership is often the development of controls which are independent of the formal organisational structure. Controls may be exerted, for example, by the internal communication system; by a charismatic leader; by selective recruitment; and through training requirements.

K. Smith: see p. 81.

L. Smith and D. Jones (eds), *Deprivation, Participation and Community Action*, Routledge and Kegan Paul, 1981.

In presenting nine case studies, this book explores some of the issues raised for community workers who wish to encourage participation. These issues include fears of co-option and unnecessary delays, accountability of community workers, and disparities of power between local people and local authorities.

Contributors include M. Taylor on the development of federations of neighbourhood groups and B. Symonds on the task of community workers in developing community-controlled structures.

T. Smithin and D. Sims, 'Ubi Caritas? – Modelling beliefs about Charities', *European Journal of Operational Research*, 10, 1982, pp. 237–243.

This article describes an application of operational research techniques to an issue concerning the voluntary sector. It concerns a project which 'explored with a number of officers from different charities their beliefs about charitable giving, and built explicit models of their beliefs so that they might be examined in a more systematic way'. Officers were enabled to learn about their own 'wisdom' and share it with others.

T. Smithin and D. Sims, 'When you can't see the Wood for the Trees', *Voluntary Action*, Spring, 1983, pp. 29–30.

This article speculates about possible ways of tackling two management problems in the voluntary sector – dealing with volunteers and 'means displacing ends'.

G. Smolka, 'Charity Law: A Case for Reform?' *NCVO Information Service*, April 1982, pp. 15–18.

This article distinguishes three important aspects of the debate about reforming charity law: the definition of a charity; permissible political activity of charities; and the operation of the Charity Commissioners.

G. Smolka: see p. 68.

R. Snaith: see p. 12.

G. S. Snell, 'The Charity Management Consultant', *Social Service Quarterly*, 45, 4, April-June 1972, pp. 127–130.

This article describes distinctive features of charities which make the task of the management consultant to charities different from consultancy work in private or public companies.

Economic and quantifiable criteria of achievement may be insufficient or non-existent, and there must be sensitivity to the motivations of people involved in running charities. A balance must be maintained between the robust independence of local voluntary committees and the desire of full-time administrators for 'well-organised central administration and control'.

In evaluating effectiveness, the present activities of the charity must be compared with an assessment of what needs to be done in the contemporary world.

A. Stanton, *Collective Working in the Personal Social Services: A Study with Nine Agencies*, M.Sc. Thesis, Cranfield Institute of Technology, 1983.

This thesis describes and analyses examples of collective working in the personal social services.

The opening chapters examine some of the ideas which have inspired collective working, including the communes and 'alternative' institutions of the 1960s, socialist and feminist writings of the 1970s, and liberal critiques of the state welfare system such as that by *Hadley and Hatch, 1981*.

Using a collaborative research method, Stanton studied nine agencies which were working collectively. Members of agencies were invited to discuss, criticise and modify the initial descriptions and to become 'co-investigators and co-researchers'. The extent to which the agencies studied used group decision-making, pooling of skills and knowledge, and task sharing, was found to vary considerably.

The author does not attempt to summarise or reach any conclusions but his final chapter picks out 'issues which suggest fruitful further discussion'. These include the fact that men are frequently excluded from collectives on the assumption that they are unable to share; the debate about whether collective working is appropriate only for small groups; and the possibility that collective working is more suitable for some tasks than others.

A. Stanton, *Windows on Collective Working*, Department of Social Policy, Cranfield Institute of Technology, 1984 (1).

This booklet is a revised edition of a questionnaire on collective working used in the author's earlier research (*Stanton, 1983*). The questions are grouped under theme headings including decision-making, pay and conditions, ideology and politics, users and accountability, and quality control. A series of quotations under each theme is provided 'to illustrate, provoke, amuse and generally flesh out the questions'.

A. Stanton, 'Collectives out of the Closet', *MDU Bulletin* 3/4, July 1984, pp. 4–5 (2).

In this article Stanton points out that, although collective working in welfare is often regarded as a 'holy grail', there are in fact numerous examples already in existence. Workers in collective teams can avoid conflict with outsiders by making clear their practice on issues such as accountability and control. Conversely, sympathetic outsiders working with collective groups must learn to respect the idea of self-management and to 'collaborate as peers with workers'.

E. Stanton, *Clients come last: Volunteers and Welfare Organisations*, Sage Publications, Beverley Hills, 1970. (ILL)

Using her participant observation study of a local chapter of the National Association for Mental Health, the author of this book describes 'the public relations effects and performance routines by which a private philanthropic social agency attempts to fabricate an image acceptable to its environment'.

The author argues that such image manipulation is especially likely to arise in agencies whose beneficiaries are stigmatised. Instead of asking volunteers to commit themselves to the agency's true goals, an appeal is made to individuals'

96

needs for status and enjoyment. Volunteer governors recruited in this way are the formal locus of authority, but are not in fact able to accomplish the agency's goals. Paid staff take on the 'defaulted responsibilities' in 'ghost roles', while trying to ensure that the image of volunteer participation is maintained.

Although staff originally perceive image manipulation as a temporary means of achieving goals in a hostile environment, the ultimate effect is 'goal displacement' and a decrease in opportunities for those individuals who want real involvement.

This book attempts to provide a theoretical explanation of two common problems of voluntary agency organisation; namely, methods of recruiting and involving members of governing bodies and the need to avoid displacement of goals. Like *Gouldner*, the author draws attention to the discrepancy between the formal and actual distribution of responsibilities in voluntary agencies.

G. Stewart (compiler), *Personal Social Services Bibliography*, Department of Social Administration, University of Lancaster, 1980 (2nd Edition).

Sections 40 and 41 of this volume contain references about voluntary agencies and volunteers working in the personal social services field.

A. Subramanian, *Designing Development Programmes: Some Pointers from Voluntary Agencies*, Working Paper 435, Indian Institute of Management, Ahmedabad, 1982.

This paper recounts a study of managerial choices and responses made by voluntary agencies in Indian development programmes.

A. Subramanian, *From Campus to Community-Building: Changing Perspectives and Programmes of Development Agencies*, Working Paper 452, Indian Institute of Management, Ahmedabad, 1983.

This paper analyses the organisational problems encountered in changing to a 'community-building' approach by two 'campus agencies', that is, ones concerned with their own survival and growth which provide welfare services for the community.

M. Tambor, 'Unions and Voluntary Agencies', *Social Work*, July, 1973, pp. 41–47.

This article discusses the implications for employing agencies (governmental and voluntary) of the growth of unionisation among social workers in the United States.

M. Taylor, 'The Development of User Management in Area Resource Centres', in B. Knight (ed), *Management in Voluntary Organisations*, Occasional Paper No. 6, ARVAC, 1984.

This paper describes how 'user' management committees were developed in four of the earliest Area Resource Centres funded by the Home Office. The composition of committees and their needs for training are discussed.

P. Taylor: see p. 52.

T. Taylor: see p. 14.

L. Taylor-Harrington: see p. 37.

T. J. R. Thomas, *'The Voluntary Body as an Employing Organisation. An Enquiry into the Role of the Officer-in-Charge of an Alcoholic Rehabilitation Centre Managed by the Methodist West London Mission'*, M.A. Dissertation, Brunel University, 1981.

The focus of this research report is the relationship between a person designated 'Officer-in-Charge' of an alcoholic rehabilitation centre and his staff and management committee.

As regards the Officer-in-Charge's relationship with staff, there was found to be no agreement as to whether he was their manager/controller, a leader by personal example, or first among equals. There was doubt also about the relative role of the Centre's house committee. Was it supposed to restrict itself to support and advice or did it have managerial and policy development functions? Many of these ambiguities could be attributed, in turn, to lack of clarity about the policy and purposes of the centre.

Lack of agreement about the role of the Officer-in-Charge was found to cause friction and unpleasantness among staff; confusion amongst members of the house committee; and inconsistencies in operating policies when the person occupying the Officer-in-Charge role changed. It was not clear to whom the staff were accountable for the quality of their work.

The researcher concludes by drawing attention to the relationship between the values embodied in a voluntary agency and its organisational structure. In the case of the alcoholic rehabilitation centre, for example, consideration of the appropriate role of staff individually and as a group, needed to be related to whether Christian mission values, a medical model of treatment of alcoholism, or broad social welfare values were the dominant operating objectives.

This small scale empirical study lends weight to the more impressionistic writings by practitioners and journalists about the realities of everyday organisational problems experienced in voluntary agencies. (See, for example, *G. J. Murray, 1969, N. Murray, 1981* and *Walsh*). It also confirms hypotheses of North American writers about lack of clarity in the policies and goals of voluntary agencies. (See, for example, *Bjur* and *McGill and Wooten, 1975 (2)*).

The study demonstrates, in addition, the possible inter-relationship between goal unclarity, the role of governing bodies and the work of service-delivering staff.

M. Thompson: see p. 24.

M. D. Tidball, *The Structure and Organisation of National Charitable Institutions with special reference to Fund-raising and the use of Volunteers,* **M.Sc. Thesis, University of Manchester, 1973.**

The purpose of this study was to examine the structure and methods of operation of the largest national charities with a view to identifying the organisational reasons for fund-raising successes. Ten charities were studied. All had incomes in excess of £1 million and raised funds through similar methods.

Many organisational factors were found to be associated with high income growth including long-term planning and firm financial control over operational activities and expenditure patterns. A strong central organisation with a supportive field force and control over units was usual. The most succesful organisations were self-aware, interested in their supporters and keen to provide a strong national image. They were likely to recruit young graduates rather than ex-servicemen and to put an emphasis on training.

The author points out that there is no relationship between worthiness of aims and fund-raising success. Poor fund-raising has an organisational cause.

The search for effectiveness in the voluntary sector has been the concern of several writers, for example, *Gerard, 1983* and *Handy, 1981*. This is one of the few published studies in the U.K. which seeks to go beyond descriptions and to identify the *organisational factors* which may contribute to 'success'.

R. J. Tollyfield and D. Pitt Francis, 'Keeping Charities off the Rocks', *Administrator*, **July 1984, pp. 10–12.**

Using the results of their own research into charity accounting, the authors of this article draw attention to a dilemma faced by small charities.

If small charities expand their operations in order to become more economically viable, they need more expertise. But if staff numbers increase and the level of donations does not keep pace, the charities appear to be 'overspending' on administration and they risk losing support. The authors' suggested solutions include the use of temporary, part-time, voluntary and seconded staff; a plan for expansion to an optimum size only; and the use of computers as a substitute for permanent staff.

J. E. Tsouderos, 'Organizational Growth', in W. A. Glaser and D. L. Sills (eds), _The Government of Associations_, Bedminster Press, Totowa, New Jersey, 1966. (ILL); and J. E. Tsouderos, 'Organizational Change in Terms of a Series of Selected Variables', _American Sociological Review_, 20, 2, April 1955, pp. 206–210.

This paper summarises some of the findings of a study of organisational growth in small voluntary associations. Five quantitative variables were subjected to time series analysis: annual income, annual expenditure, value of property, annual membership figures and number of administrative employees.

The study showed that, in general, 'there is a definite functional relationship between the growth in membership of an association and other variables'. Moreover, voluntary associations have a tendency to increase their membership to a certain point and then reach a maximum growth and this maximum membership itself declines over time. But when membership declines there is no immediate decline in income and there is a 'tendency for the process of formalization to continue in the period when the social group contracts'.

The author presents a number of tentative propositions, which seek to explain some of the observed relationships between variables and the observed cycle of growth and formalisation. For example, it is suggested that associations which serve very specific interests may have a maximum size in any given area; that as an association meets a need in an area, its membership may correspondingly decrease; and that increased membership brings increased heterogeneity of interests and therefore lays the basis for conflict and a decline in membership in the future.

J. E. Tsouderos: see also p. 25.

D. J. Tucker, 'Senior Management and the Co-ordination of Services', _Social Work Research and Abstracts_, 1980, pp. 11–18.

This article arises from the argument that efficiency and effectiveness in social work agencies (which are mainly non-statutory organisations in North America) could be enhanced by co-ordination of service delivery. It reports an investigation into whether such co-ordination is increased by senior management involvement in 'inter-organisational activity', including involvement in the governing boards of other organisations, inter-organisational group meetings and inter-organisational case conferences. Structured interviews were conducted with senior managers of seventeen social service organisations (both statutory and voluntary) in Toronto.

The findings suggested that inter-organisational activity is inversely related to co-ordination. Senior managers used the additional information obtained through involvement in inter-organisational activity to exert increased control over their own organisations and to restrict co-operative interchanges with other organisations.

The author concludes that perhaps co-ordination of agencies' work needs to be done by a 'hierarchically superior and authoritative body'.

D. J. Tucker, 'Voluntary Auspices and the Behaviour of Social Services Organisations', *Social Service Review*, December 1981, pp. 603–627.

This article reports a Canadian study of voluntary social service agencies that is, agencies run under voluntary, rather than statutory or public, auspices. The starting point of the enquiry was the proposition that voluntary social services organisations are relatively 'insecure vis-à-vis their environments' because they operate in an illiberal, hostile context and lack 'a legal mandate and guaranteed access to public funds'. It is suggested that organisations which are insecure 'evince characteristics which differentiate them from more secure organisations'.

Seven hypotheses were deduced from this proposition and tested using quantified data from 17 voluntary organisations. Voluntary control was not found to be positively associated with a selective approach to clients. However, it was positively associated with organisational adaptiveness and involvement of senior managers in bargaining activities with other voluntary organisations; both of which may be seen as aids to organisational survival. Voluntary control was negatively associated with extent of organisational involvement in co-ordination and an individualised approach to service provision. As regards centralisation of authority and usage of rules to guide employee behaviour, curvilinear relationships were found; that is, 'as an organization's security vis-à-vis its environment increases, its use of rules increases and a decentralization of authority occurs'. But this is reversed beyond a certain stage.

This study which focuses on the environment within which voluntary agencies operate may be compared with the broader studies by *Gerard, 1983*, and *Kramer, 1981*, which also sought to identify distinctive organisational features.

J. Turner, 'Voluntary Rations', *New Society*, 13 July 1978, p. 75.

This article discusses the bid by NCSS (now NCVO) to control and channel central government funds to local intermediary bodies, following the report of the *Wolfenden Committee*. But the more radical of the local intermediary bodies (Councils for Voluntary Service and Rural Community Councils) wanted to break away from NCSS.

The author also draws attention to the fear that CVS could act as a barrier to statutory funding of non-conformist voluntary agencies.

101

A. C. Twelvetrees, *Community Associations and Centres: A Comprehensive Study*, Pergamon Press, 1976.

The study described in this book was an attempt to shed light 'on how community associations work in practice, what difficulties they come up against and how those difficulties may sometimes be overcome'. Associations were studied in four areas of Edinburgh where there existed a purpose-built community centre provided by the Education Department.

The variety of aims, sometimes mutually conflicting, of community associations were found to raise problems for both members and professional helpers. Associations were often 'expected to be a federal organisation at representative level and yet to meet community needs directly at the grassroots level, fostering the growth of individual membership'.

The twin aims raised problems of organisational structure. The function of co-ordination and the responsibility for a large building tended to produce and demand formal bureaucratic structures but these were not conducive to individual involvement and identification with the association.

Difficulties also arose over the activities of associations. There was a tendency to concentrate on boosting membership and serving individual, local needs, even after other organisations had grown up to meet the needs more effectively. Identification and meeting of wider community needs and co-ordination of community activities tended to be neglected.

The author concludes that community associations should aim to meet only those needs which other local organisations fail to satisfy. A secondary co-ordinating association is the only 'true' community association; a 'primary' community association is not distinguishable from other community groups.

The practical problems of implementing unclear and incompatible goals emerge clearly from this study. The difficulty of combining co-ordinative aims with other purposes was noted also by *Lansley, 1976* and *Leat et al, 1981*.

J. Unell, *Voluntary Social Services: Financial Resources*, Bedford Square Press/NCVO, 1979.

This booklet derives from a study in which the financial reserves of a sample of national, service-giving, voluntary organisations were compared within the five-year period 1970/71 to 1975/76.

J. Unell: see p. 68.

K. Urwin: see p. 31.

B. Utting, 'Personal Care by Government Purchase: Lessons from the American Experience', *Social Work Service*, Autumn 1982, pp. 25–30.

This article discusses the author's impression of the United States system of personal social services provision. It focuses on the widely-used system whereby U.S. government agencies buy personal social services from independent (i.e. voluntary and commercial) contractors rather than provide them directly themselves. This system is now 'a subject of lively controversy' in the United States. Services may be purchased in bulk or, as is more usual in Social Services Departments in England at present, on an *ad hoc* basis for individual clients. 'The essence of purchase as a policy, however, is to give the process the form and clarity of a negotiated and binding agreement.'

The arguments in favour of purchase are summarised as 'the presumed greater economy and efficiency' of the independent sector, 'its flexibility of response, its adaptiveness to changing needs and its capacity to provide service in a form that the clients find more acceptable'. But Utting says that there is evidence to set against these arguments. The independent sector can sometimes exceed government in rigidity; saving of public money may be short-term only; private monopoly is no more attractive than public monopoly of service provision; and the purchase system can give rise to wheeling and dealing not far removed from corruption as agencies strive to win and to retain contracts.

For non-profit or voluntary welfare agencies problems may arise if they become dependent for their survival on public money. The purchase system may also oblige them to be more politically active and more overtly, financially accountable to the public.

Utting concludes by discussing the range of services which, in England, could conceivably be met by independent agencies in purchase agreements with statutory agencies. But he points out that purchase policies contain conflicting values of caring for human needs and cost consciousness. Nevertheless, 'systematic purchase policies might offer agencies outside the public sector a better chance of survival'.

W. van der Eyken, *Home-Start*, Home-Start Consultancy, 1983.

This book is an evaluation of the period 1974–78 of the Leicestershire Home-Start Scheme. The Scheme uses volunteers to work with mothers and families, mainly referred from the statutory sector. The volunteers are supported by a paid organiser and the costs are borne by the social services department.

Voluntary Action (This journal was amalgamated with *New Society* in October 1985.)

This journal deals with issues concerning or related to the voluntary sector. It was published quarterly by NCVO up to 1983. As from January 1984, 10 issues per year are planned.

Voluntary Action, 'Opening Up: All in a Good Cause?', *Voluntary Action*, **Winter, 1981, pp. 3–4. (No author named.)**

This article reports on and discusses some of the well-publicised disputes which had recently occurred in voluntary agencies. The article focuses on MIND, Gingerbread and Amnesty International. The writer suggests that although staff may be committed to the cause of their agency and willing to work for low pay, they are less willing to tolerate bad management practice. The growing unionisation of the voluntary sector is discussed.

Voluntary Action, 'Opening Up: Identity Crisis in the RSPCA Worsened by Money Troubles', *Voluntary Action*, **Autumn, 1982, p. 3. (No author named.)**

This is a short note recounting the pressures within a large national voluntary agency towards changes of goals and methods of work. Problems caused by over-expansion are also discussed.

Voluntary Action Leadership

This is a quarterly journal from the United States about organising volunteers and voluntary action. Subscriptions are available from 'Volunteer', National Centre for Citizen Involvement, 1111 North 19th Street, Room 500, Arlington, VA 22209, U.S.A.

Voluntary Action Westminster (VAW), *Management 1: Organisational Structure and Charitable Status*, **VAW, 1982.**

This leaflet describes the legal formats or 'constitutional choices' available to voluntary agencies and some aspects of charitable status.

Voluntary Action Westminster, *Management 2: Voluntary Organisations as Employers*, **VAW, 1983.**

This leaflet outlines the legal obligations that management committees have as employers and points out how legal requirements overlap with good practice.

Voluntary Forum Abstracts

A quarterly abstracts journal published by NCVO and the Volunteer Centre.

104

Voluntary Services Unit: see p. 54.

Volunteer Centre, *Research into Voluntary Involvement: Papers given at a day conference at King's Fund Centre, London, December, 1977*, Volunteer Centre, 1978.

Many of the papers in this booklet were contributed by authors whose works relevant to organisation and management issues have appeared elsewhere and are referenced in this bibliography. In addition, there are papers by F. Armstrong and S. Otto on action research in voluntary agencies, and by D. Horton Smith outlining the main areas of North American research into voluntary action.

L. E. Waddilove, *Foundations and Trusts – Innovations or Survivals?*, Eileen Younghusband Lecture, National Institute for Social Work, 1979.

This lecture defines the purposes of foundations and trusts and raises some issues about their current role in social welfare provision.

M. Walker, 'Charity Goes on the Dole', *The Guardian*, 30 March 1983. p. 13.

This article reports on three voluntary agencies which have the 'haunting flavour of Victorian philanthropy' – the Peabody Trust, Dr Barnardo's and the Shaftesbury Society. The way in which the agencies have adapted to current needs and problems is described.

H. W. Wallender: see p. 79.

L. Walsh, 'How to Ruin a Voluntary Organisation', *MDU Bulletin*, 2, September 1983, pp. 3–4.

Using his experience as a consultant in 'organisation effectiveness', the author outlines some of the many ways in which workers in voluntary agencies can 'ruin' their agencies. These negative activities fall into two categories: those which separate the organisation from 'its community, users, clients and environment', and those which split the organisation itself 'so that it ceases to function'. Walsh concludes that voluntary agencies must learn to deal with their real problems by developing processes 'by which they will not only identify and deal with their troubles but also get closer to their communities'.

A. Webb, *Collective Action and Welfare Pluralism*, ARVAC, 1981.

This paper provides a critical analysis of the concept of 'gradualist welfare pluralism' as proposed by *Gladstone, 1979*.

A. Webb: see p. 43.

A. Webb, L. Day and D. Weller, *Voluntary Social Service Manpower Resources*, Personal Social Services Council, London, 1976. (A limited number of copies are on sale at NISW.)

This paper sets out the results of a small exploratory study of the manpower and training resources of 44 voluntary organisations in the personal social services field.

Unpaid workers were involved not only in fund-raising, but also in policy-making and management, agency-maintenance activities and all kinds of field-work with clients. A backlog of training needs was found for volunteers, staff who train volunteers and professional staff – and the authors suggest that the problems of voluntary organisations in providing training for their staff would be eased if the national educational system would bear the cost of training personal social services staff, as for other professionals. Voluntary organisations' difficulties in recruitment were found to be due to competition from the public sector with regard to wages, career structure and organisational support.

The authors conclude that, since resources are so scarce, voluntary agencies should not be obliged to provide services which supplement or substitute for statutory services, at the expense of pursuing their own specialist and innovative functions, which complement statutory provision.

A. Webb and G. Wistow, *Whither State Welfare? Policy and Implementation in the Personal Social Services 1979–80*, Royal Institute of Public Administration, London, 1982.

This brief review of social policy implementation includes a discussion of the risks and ambiguities of a policy of welfare pluralism or a 'mixed economy of welfare'.

J. Weber, *Managing the Board of Directors*, Greater New York Fund, New York, 1975. (ILL)

This is a manual about what the author regards as the requisite functions of boards of directors (governing bodies) of voluntary agencies.

Weber begins by distinguishing six basic elements of agency operations – administration, finance, personnel management, 'programme development', public relations, and community relations. He suggests that boards should be organised around these elements and should be given relevant functions to perform according to their expertise. They should thus, be led to understand that their purpose is business rather than social.

Referring to the relationship between boards and staff in voluntary agencies, Weber says, 'Effective board-staff relations begin with a clear and common understanding of both board members and staff as to the precise purpose of the

106

organisation, its service goals and how the organisation proposes to reach and serve clients effectively.' He suggests that 'Board-staff relations are frequently hampered because of the difficulty encountered by board and staff re understanding the difference between policy formulation and administration.'

The problematic relationship between *staff and governing bodies* has been widely noted in the literature (for example in *Feek, 1982* (1), *Kramer, 1981*, and *Leat et al, 1981*). Weber's practical approach to the problem of how functions should and might be allocated and shared is similar to that of *Conrad and Glenn* and may be contrasted with the more sociological explanations of, for example, *Gouldner* and *Senor*.

J. Weber, 'The BBB Project: building better boards', *Voluntary Action Leadership*, Winter 1983, pp. 20–21.

This article describes a project to establish a network of 100 community colleges in the United States that will offer a regular curriculum of training for voluntary board (i.e. management committee) members. Favourite topics for courses include fund-raising, board/staff relationships, management skills and leadership.

J. Weber: see p. 47 and p. 48.

D. A. Webster, *Local Voluntary Organisations*, Social Services Department, Doncaster Metropolitan Borough Council, undated.

This is a local profile of voluntary agencies; a study of the nature and needs of voluntary organisations operating in the personal social services field in the Metropolitan District of Doncaster.

B. A. Weisbrod, *The Voluntary Non-profit Sector: An Economic Analysis*, Lexington Books, Lexington, Mass., 1977.

This book provides an analysis of the role of the third (non-governmental and not-for-profit) sector in the economy of the United States, as a provider of 'collective consumption goods'.

D. Weller: see p. 106.

E. G. Wertheim, 'Evolution of Structure and Process in Voluntary Organizations: A Study of Thirty-Five Consumer Food Cooperatives', *Journal of Voluntary Action Research*, 5, 1, 1976, pp. 4–15.

This article examines how individual and organisational factors influence the transformation of structure in non-profit food-buying co-operatives.

B. Whitaker, *The Foundations*, Eyre Methuen, 1974.

This book provides a personal, largely impressionistic, review of the activities of foundations in the United States and Britain. Topics covered include the motives of founders; policy in dispensing funds; CIA infiltration; and the art of grantmanship. The author gives his views on appropriate pioneering roles for foundations.

G. Williams, *Inner City Policy: A Partnership with the Voluntary Sector?*, NCVO Occasional Paper 3, Bedford Square Press/NCVO, 1983.

Using Manchester as an example, this book examines the experiences of voluntary agencies and local authorities in working together on Inner City partnership schemes. It is noted that the organisational survival of voluntary agencies demands clear structures and procedures in partnership schemes. The failure of Councils of Voluntary Service to achieve a major co-ordinating role for the voluntary sector is also discussed.

G. Wistow: see p. 106.

Wolfenden Committee Report, *The Future of Voluntary Organisations*, Croom Helm, 1978.

This is the report of a committee appointed by the Joseph Rowntree Memorial Trust and Carnegie U.K. Trust 'to review the role and functions of voluntary organisations in the U.K. over the next twenty-five years'.

The report begins by reviewing the relationship between the voluntary sector and the three other sectors concerned with meeting need; namely, informal networks, the statutory sector, and the commercial system. It notes the organisational diversity of the voluntary sector and the fact that its total manpower resources (staff plus volunteers) exceed those of the statutory sector. The roles and functions that voluntary organisations could and do perform are discussed, along with the limitations of the sector which include its unevenness, diversity, specificity and small financial resources.

Four chapters are devoted to discussion of the relation between voluntary organisations and other bodies, including central government, local government and the intermediary bodies which provide support for individual voluntary agencies.

Three 'widely acceptable' propositions about voluntary agencies, that they are accountable, independent and effective, are discussed. Accountability, it is suggested, is not a problem in practice but the demands of funders for control may conflict with the traditional independence of voluntary organisations. Problems of effectiveness and efficiency may arise in voluntary organisations, especially over adapting to changing circumstances and needs, avoiding duplication of services, and monitoring quality. The committee suggested that independent intermediary bodies might be helpful in solving these kinds of problems.

The report concludes that there is 'a strong case' for building up training facilities which take account of the fact that the 'ethos and problems of voluntary organisations are in some respect different from those found in the statutory and commercial sectors'. The need to develop professional and managerial expertise in the sector is stressed.

The Wolfenden Committee Report stands as a landmark among the recent UK literature. It provided an overview of the voluntary sector and its inter-relationships with other sectors, and also raised issues about the internal working and effectiveness of individual agencies. Some of the challenges for training presented by the report were picked up by the *Handy Committee, 1981*.

W. Wolfensberger, *The Third Stage in the Evolution of Voluntary Associations for the Mentally Retarded*, National Institute on Mental Retardation, Toronto, 1973. (ILL)

The theme of this booklet is that voluntary associations evolve in a relatively predictable manner which is 'subject to certain laws of psychology and sociology' and that, therefore, they are subject to predictable problems and solutions. Young organisations can learn from mature ones and associations in 'advanced stages' can reorientate themselves with respect to their routine functions and priorities.

Three stages in the growth of voluntary associations for the mentally retarded are distinguished by Wolfensberger.

The origin of such agencies is often in evidence of lack of services or of professional neglect. Parents found the agency and its first stage is 'provision of services'.

Gradually service needs grow and a feeling develops that these should be public services. So the second stage of growth is getting other bodies to fund and operate services. This, however, gives rise to uncertainty about the goals of the organisation and difficulties in retaining members. On the other hand, if agencies retain their 'provision' functions at this stage they may face problems of administration and maintaining vigour. The problem is to simultaneously 'max-

109

imise the rights of the retarded' and protect the association's own existence. This requires an acceptance and understanding of 'systematic organisational phenomena' and the institution of 'systematic organisational safeguards' to ensure 'ultimate goals' are maintained.

The third stage of growth is said to be 'change agentry' which involves 'bringing about adaptive changes on behalf of mentally retarded', for example, by demonstration of a service or promotion of research.

Like *Chapin and Tsouderos* and *Katz*, Wolfensberger attempts to provide a *theoretical explanation* for growth; although he concentrates on *changes in goals* accompanying growth rather than on moves towards formalisation and bureaucratisation.

L. Wooten: see p. 72 (two entries).

M. S. Wortman, 'A Radical Shift from Bureaucracy to Strategic Management in Voluntary Organizations', *Journal of Voluntary Action Research*, **10, 1, 1981, pp. 62–81.**

This article argues that all organisations go through predictable stages of development and that voluntary agencies should consider ways of speeding up their development process in order to avoid some of their well-documented organisational problems.

P. Wright, 'Should the Salt of the Earth be Managed?' *MDU Bulletin*, **I, May 1983, pp. 1–2.**

This article introduces the first issue of the *MDU Bulletin*. It acknowledges the scepticism that exists about applying management to voluntary agencies, but argues that 'voluntary organisations do need to develop their own forms of competence'. Organisational issues tend to become visible in voluntary agencies in a destructive way at the point where organisation breaks down. The *MDU Bulletin* aims 'to help bring the organisational issues facing voluntary agencies into view in a more positive way'.

R. Wright: see p. 19.

Yale Program of Nonprofit Organizations, *Research Reports*, **Institution for Social and Policy Studies, Yale University, 1981 onwards.**

Research Reports is an occasional publication of Yale University's Program on Nonprofit Organizations. It reports on the progress, or the results, of research conducted under the Program's auspices. (Enquiries direct to Yale University.)

Yale Program of Nonprofit Organizations, *Working Papers*, Institution for Social and Policy Studies, Yale University. (Some copies available for inspection at NCVO Library.)

The Yale Program has published a number of *Working Papers* in the general area of organisation and management.

S. Yeo, *Religion and Voluntary Organisations in Crisis*, Croom Helm, 1976.

This is a case study of social welfare provision in Reading at the turn of this century, focusing on the role of religious and voluntary groups and on the social consequences of capitalism.

T. Yeo, *Public Accountability and Regulation of Charities: The Case for Reform*, the Spastics Society, 1983.

This pamphlet provides a brief description of the characteristics of charities and sets out 'a simple programme designed to improve the public accountability of charities and to introduce a firm system of regulation'. Accountability could be improved through compulsory filing of charities' annual accounts, widening of access to the AGMs of charities, and the development of a code of practice for fund-raising and administrative costs. The case is also argued for the establishment of a 'Charity Council' – an instrument of self-regulation which 'can act as a reference point for determining what constitutes charitable activity, which can scrutinise the formation of new charities and which can deal with complaints or criticisms about the operations of existing charities'.

Young Volunteer Resources Unit, *Working with Your Management Committee*, National Youth Bureau, 1979.

The main aim of this booklet is 'to help analyse obstacles and work through problems that may inhibit mutually constructive and useful relations' between workers in voluntary youth organisations and their management committees.

It begins by examining and making some practical suggestions about the expectations, responsibilities and roles of both workers and management committees. It emphasises that the relation between workers and management committees is in many respects negotiable and 'can involve a delicate balance of support and control, consultation and decision-making'.

A second chapter, on the structuring of management committees, stresses the importance of a clearly-defined constitution for voluntary agencies. The respective roles of chairmen and women, workers, and volunteers on committees are discussed. Subsequent chapters examine training needs of committee members and technical and procedural aspects of running meetings. The booklet concludes with some case studies.

The need for voluntary agency staff to support their management committees

111

and help them develop their role is a recurrent theme throughout the booklet. An active and involved management committee, it is argued, brings benefits to all parts of the agency.

This U.K. contribution to the practical literature on the functions of management committees may be compared with the more detailed U.S. studies of *Hartogs and Weber, 1974*, and *Conrad and Glenn*.

M. N. Zald, 'Organizations as Polities: An Analysis of Community Organization Agencies', in R. M. Kramer and M. Specht (eds), *Readings in Community Organization Practice*, Prentice Hall, Englewood Cliffs, New Jersey, 1969.

Using organisational analysis, this paper presents some concepts about the structure of community organisations, with a view to explaining 'some of the determinants of agency processes'.

Four inter-related concepts form the core of the analysis. First, there is the constitution of the organisation, its basic zones of activity, goals and norms of procedure and relationships. Zald argues that the goals of community organisations can be classified according to three dimensions: change or service orientation; institution or individual and group orientation; member or external orientation.

A second important analytic concept is the constituency and resource base of the organisation; the groups and individuals who control the organisation and to whom the executive core of the agency is most immediately responsible. Zald suggests that, 'To the extent that an agency is heavily dependent on its constituency, it is likely to develop a constitution giving little room for discretion.' Constituency-agency relationships are crucial in determining the extent of the paid director's role in agency decision-making.

A third important concept is that of the target population which the community organisation wishes to affect. Fourth, community agencies have external relations that can 'facilitate, impede, or be neutral to the accomplishment of their goals'.

Zald proposes several testable propositions about the conditions under which different kinds of community organisational problems and processes may arise. He argues that organisational analysis 'will be valuable for both sociology and community organisation practice'.

The significance of this article lies in the development of concepts which are related to organisational problems. It may be compared with other attempts to develop *typologies and theories* of voluntary organisations (see, for example, *Johnson, 1978 (1)*).

Users' Guide to Topics and Issues

This section is not a comprehensive index of the works cited. Its purpose is to draw together some initial references for those readers who wish to explore particular topics and organisational issues.

Accountability   Judge
                                  Kramer, 1979 (2)
                                  Rowe
                                  Smith and Hague
                                  T. Yeo
and independence   *see* Funding
and organisation   Rowe
                                  Lenn, 1982
for work   G. Smith
                                  Thomas
public   Austin and Posnett
                                  Fizdale
                                  Marshall
                                  Mullin
to funders   Berg and Wright
                                  Hartogs and Weber, 1978
                                  Hatch and Mocroft, 1983
                                  Judge
                                  Rowe
                                  Rosenbaum
Bureaucratisation   *see* Growth
Care – formal and informal   Abrams, 1978 (1)
                                  Richardson and Goodman
Case Studies   Billis, 1984 (2)
                                  Donnison *et al*
                                  Hadley *et al*
                                  Hatch and Mocroft, 1983
                                  James
                                  Jerman
                                  Lansley, 1976
                                  Leat *et al*
                                  Lenn, 1972

Case Studies *cont.*

Lovelock
Seyd, 1975
Seyd, 1976
D. Sills, 1957
Thomas

Central Offices   *see* Headquarters
Change   *see* Growth and Innovation
Charity Commissioners   Marshall
Collective working   A. Stanton
Committees
  functions   Conrad and Glenn
  systems   Conrad and Glenn
Conflict
  resolution   Donnison *et al*
Contracts
  purchase of service   *see* POSC
Co-ordination
  between voluntary organisations   Lansley, 1976
Leat *et al*
McKee
Tucker, 1980

Costs
  comparisons with statutory   Hartogs and Weber, 1978
    sector   Hatch and Mocroft, 1979
Councils of Voluntary Service   *see* Intermediary bodies
Director   *see* Staff
Effectiveness
  in management   *see* Management
  organisational   Tidball
Wolfenden

Employment
  conditions   Burns
Formalisation   *see* Growth and Informality
Funders
  accountability to   *see* Accountability
Funding
  and costs   Hartogs and Weber, 1978
Hatch and Mocroft, 1983
  and goals   *see* Goals
  and independence   Judge
Kramer, 1966
Kramer, 1979 (2)
Rice

Funding
  and independence *cont.*
  by government

  by local authorities

  fundraising
  of projects
Goals
  and funding

  and organisational structure

  definition of/change of/
    confusion

  multiple

Governing Bodies
  and staff

Smith and Hague
Wolfenden
see Statutory authorities and
    POSC
see Statutory authorities and
    POSC
Tidball
Berg and Wright

Berg and Wright
Hartogs and Weber, 1978
Kramer, 1979 (1)
Kramer, 1981
Rosenbaum
Tidball
Abrams, 1981
Acton
Lansley, 1976
Twelvetrees
Donnison *et al*
Hadley *et al*
Hyman
James
McGill and Wooten, 1975 (2)
McKee
National Federation of Housing
    Associations
E. Stanton
Thomas
Twelvetrees
Wolfensberger
Bjur
Leat *et al*
Twelvetrees

Arnold *et al*
Bennett
Connors, 1980 (2)
Conrad and Glenn
Fizdale
Gouldner
Griffiths *et al*
Harris

Governing Bodies and staff *cont.*	Hartogs and Weber, 1974 Kramer, 1965 Kramer, 1981 Senor Thomas Weber, 1975 Young Volunteer Resources Unit
functions and responsibilities	Association of Metropolitan Authorities (AMA) Connors, 1980 (2) Conrad and Glenn Feek, 1982 (1) Harris Hartogs and Weber, 1974 Kahn Kramer, 1981 Lovelock Weber, 1975 Young Volunteer Resources Unit
membership	AMA, etc Hartogs and Weber, 1974 Kramer, 1965 Kramer, 1981 Mullin E. Stanton
types	Harris McKee
Government	*see* Statutory authorities
Growth	Berg and Wright Chapin and Tsouderos Hadley *et al* Hyman Jerman King National Federation of Housing Associations Wolfensberger Wortman
and bureaucratisation	Billis, 1984 (1) Chapin and Tsouderos Katz Kramer, 1981 Lundberg

and bureaucratisation *cont.*

and informality   Tsouderos

and informality   Billis, 1984 (1)

                                    Hyman

                                    Jerman

and planned change   Billis, 1984 (2)

                                    Lansley, 1976

origins of voluntary   Hatch, 1980 (1)

   organisations   King

                                    Rice

Headquarters

and local groups   Kramer, 1981

                                    Lenn, 1972

                                    Lovelock

                                    Richardson and Goodman

Hierarchy

alternatives   Kahle

                                    A. Stanton, 1983

Informality   *see* Care and Growth

Innovation   *see* Growth and Policy

Intermediary bodies   Lansley, 1976

                                    Leat *et al*

                                    Mullin

                                    Wolfenden

International information   Kramer, 1981

                                    Scott, 1982

Leadership   G. Smith

Local authorities   *see* Statutory authorities

Local groups

and headquarters   *see* Headquarters

Location   Hatch and Mocroft, 1977

                                    Abrams *et al*, 1981

Management

and voluntary   Billis, 1984 (1)

   organisations   Handy, 1983 (1)

effectiveness   Gerard, 1983

                                    Handy, 1981

                                    Morris

                                    Tidball

of volunteers   *see* Volunteers

style   Gerard, 1983

techniques   Borst and Montana

                                    Newman and Wallender

                                    Snell

117

Management Committees   *see* Governing bodies
Members
  participation   *see* Participation
Methodology
  study of voluntary
    organisations   Butcher *et al*
Need
  and resources   *see* Resources
Organisation
  and social policy   *see* Social policy
Organisational features
  distinctive   Donnison *et al*
                              Gerard, 1983
                              Griffiths *et al*
                              Johnson, 1981
                              Kramer, 1981
                              Lansley, 1979
                              G. J. Murray
                              Ruckle
                              Scott, 1982
                              Tucker, 1981

Organisational problems
  distinctive   Billis, 1979
                              Billis, 1984 (1)
                              Bjur
                              Gerard, 1983
                              Hadley and Hatch, 1980
                              Handy, 1981
                              Kramer, 1981
                              G. Smith

Origins
  of voluntary organisations   *see* Growth
Paid staff   *see* Staff
Participation   Chapin and Tsouderos
                              Rowe
                              E. Stanton

Policy
  and funding   *see* Goals
  and values   *see* Values
  confusion   *see* Goals
  innovation   Donnison *et al*
                              Hage and Dewar

POSC   Judge

POSC *cont.*

	Sharkansky
	Smith and Hague
	Utting

Projects
  development of ... Arnold *et al*
  and funding ... *see* Funding
Public Accountability ... *see* Accountability
Purchase of Service Contracts ... *see* POSC
Relations with other agencies ... *see* Co-ordination
Resources
  and need ... Abrams, 1978 (1)
  Abrams, *et al*, 1981
  Hadley *et al*
  Hatch and Mocroft, 1977
  Shenfield and Allen

Self-help
  and service provision ... Billis, 1984 (2)
  Jerman
  organisations ... Katz
  Richardson and Goodman

Size ... *see* Growth
Social policy
  and organisation ... Billis, 1984 (1)
  Billis, 1984 (2)
  Hatch and Mocroft, 1979
  Richardson and Goodman

Social Services Departments ... *see* Statutory authorities, relations with

Staff
  and governing body ... *see* Governing bodies
  director ... Conrad and Glenn
  Thomas
  motivation ... Lane
  Pearce
  D. H. Smith
  training ... *see* Training
Statutory authorities
  comparative costs ... *see* Costs
  funding by ... Hartogs and Weber, 1978
  Kramer, 1966
  Kramer, 1979 (2)
  NCVO, 1984
  Lovelock

Statutory authorities funding by *cont.*	Rice Rosenbaum Utting
relations with	Abrams, 1981 AMA, *et al* Cousins, 1978 Griffiths, 1981 Hatch and Mocroft, 1983 Judge Lenn, 1982 Scott, 1982 Wolfenden
Style of management	*see* Management
Theories of voluntary agencies	Billis, 1979 Billis, 1984 (1) Gordon and Babchuk Hatch, 1980 (1) Hatch, 1980 (2) Johnson, 1978 (1) Kramer, 1981 McKee Rowe Zald
organisational models	Hadley and Hatch, 1981 Kahle Ruckle
Training	AMA, etc. Gerard, 1983 Handy, 1981 Mullin Webb *et al* Wolfenden
Trustees	*see* Governing Bodies
Typologies	*see* Theories
Values	Hage and Dewar Gerard, 1983
Volunteers management of	Hadley *et al* Leat and Darvill Lenn, 1982 Shenfield and Allen

Journals Cited

The following journals and newspapers are referred to in this bibliography.

Academy of Management Review
Accountant
Administration and Social Work
Administrative Science Quarterly
Administrator
American Sociological Review
British Journal of Alcohol and Alcoholism
British Journal of Psychiatry
Charity (published by CAF)
Community Care
Community Development Journal
Current Anthropology
European Journal of Operational Research
Financial Times
The Guardian
Health and Social Services Journal
Home Office Research Bulletin
Human Organization
Information Service for Voluntary Organisations (published by Bedford Square Press/NCVO)
Journal of Social Policy
Journal of the Royal College of Physicians of London
Journal of Voluntary Action Research
Law Society Gazette
Local Government Chronicle

London Journal
London Review of Public Administration
Marriage Guidance
MDU Bulletin (published by Bedford Square Press/NCVO)
Multinational Business
National Westminster Bank Quarterly Review
New Society
Policy and Politics
Political Quarterly
Public Administration
Public Administration Review
Social Casework
Social and Economic Administration
Social Forces
Social Policy and Administration
Social Service Quarterly
Social Service Review
Social Work
Social Work Research and Abstracts
Social Work Service
Social Work Today
Voluntary Action (This journal amalgamated with *New Society* in October 1985.)
Voluntary Action Leadership
Voluntary Forum Abstracts

Useful Addresses

This guide gives the addresses of publishers of booklets and pamphlets included in the text. Some books which may not be readily available in public or academic libraries, but which are obtainable on Inter-Library Loan, are marked 'ILL' in the text.

Adam Smith Institute, PO Box 316, London SW1P 3DJ

Association of Community Workers (ACW), Colombo Street Sports and Community Centre, Colombo Street, Blackfriars, London SE1 8DP

Association of Researchers into Voluntary Action & Community Involvement (ARVAC), 26 Queens Road, Wivenhoe, Essex CO3 3PB

Calouste Gulbenkian Foundation, 98 Portland Place, London W1N 4ET

CBD Research Ltd, 154 High Street, Beckenham, Kent BR3 1EA

Centre for Interfirm Comparison, 8 West Stockwell Street, Colchester, Essex CO1 1HN

Charities Aid Foundation (CAF), 48 Pembury Road, Tonbridge, Kent TN9 2JD

DHSS Library, Alexander Fleming House, Elephant and Castle, London SE1 6BY

Directory of Social Change, 9 Mansfield Place, London NW3 1HS

Doncaster Metropolitan Borough Council, Social Services Department, Old Guildhall Yard, Frenchgate, Doncaster, South Yorkshire DN1 1RH

Economic and Social Research Council (ESRC), 1 Temple Avenue, London EC4Y 0BD

Grubb Institute, EWR Centre, Cloudesley Street, London N1 6HU

Hackney Community Action (HCA), 380 Old Street, London EC1 9LT

Home Office, 50 Queen Anne's Gate, London SW1H 9AT

Indian Institute of Management, Vastrapur, Ahmedabad – 380015, India

Institute of Chartered Accountants in England and Wales, 399 Silbury Boulevard, Witan Crate East, Central Milton Keynes MK9 2HL

Joseph Rowntree Memorial Trust, Beverley House, Shipton Road, York YO3 6RB

King's Fund Centre, 126 Albert Street, London NW1 7NF

Liverpool Council for Voluntary Service (Liverpool CVS), 14 Castle Street, Liverpool L20 NJ

London Voluntary Service Council (LVSC), 68 Chalton Street, London NW1 1JR

Manpower Services Commission (MSC), Selkirk House, 166 High Holborn, London WC1V 6PB

National Association of Youth Clubs, Keswick House, 30 Peacock Lane, Leicester LE1 5NY

National Council of Social Service (NCSS) *now* **National Council for Voluntary Organisations**

National Council for Voluntary Organisations (NCVO), 26 Bedford Square, London WC1B 3HU

National Federation of Community Organisations (NFCO), 8–9 Upper Street, London N1 0PQ

National Federation of Housing Associations (NFHA), 30–32 Southampton Street, Strand, London WC2E 7HE

National Institute for Social Work (NISW), Mary Ward House, 5–7 Tavistock Place, London WC1H 9SS

National Institute on Mental Retardation, Kinsmen NIMR Building, York University Campus, 4700 Keele Street, Downsview, Toronto, Ontario, M3J 1P3

National Youth Bureau (NYB), 17–23 Albion Street, Leicester LE1 6GD

Policy Studies Institute (PSI), 1–2 Castle Lane, London SW1E 6DR

Royal Institute of Public Administration (RIPA), 3 Birdcage Walk, London SW1H 9JJ

Social Science Research Council (SSRC) *now* **Economic and Social Research Council (ESRC),** 1 Temple Avenue, London EC4Y 0BD

Spastics Society, 12 Park Crescent, London W1N 4EQ

Voluntary Action Westminster (VAW), 1 St Mary's Terrace, London W2 1SU

Voluntary Services Unit (VSU), Queen Anne's Gate, London SW1H 9AT

Volunteer Centre, 29 Lower King's Road, Berkhamsted, Herts HP4 2AB

Yale University Program on Nonprofit Organizations, PO Box 154 Yale Station, 88 Trumbull Street, New Haven, Connecticut 06520, U.S.A.